Windy City Baby

Windy City Baby

An Insider's Guide to Raising Kids in Chicago

Shana Trombley

CURTAIN TIME PRESS

Windy City Baby
by Shana Trombley

Published by: Curtain Time Press
                 3540 North Southport, #307
                 Chicago, Illinois 60657
                 www.windycitybaby.com

ISBN: 0-9758994-0-6

Copyedit by Gail M. Kearns, To Press and Beyond, Santa Barbara, California
Cover and jacket design by Deb Voss
Book production by Penelope C. Paine
Book Design and Typography, Cirrus Design

Printed in the United States of America

The information in this guide is the latest available at the time of publication. However, businesses come and go, Web sites changes and, yes, prices increase all the time. It is always a good idea to call ahead and confirm details. While the information in this book is extensive, it is not a comprehensive list of every service provider or business in Chicago. Rather, I have included information about programs, places, stores, service providers etc. that I have had personal experience with and that I know are satisfactory and reliable. Also, the information in this book is intended to be a resource guide only. At various times I may make specific endorsements of programs, classes, stores or service providers.

For my mom who gave me the gift of time to write this book,

my husband who believed I could do it,

and most of all to Abby and Peter,

the two greatest research assistants a mom could hope for

Contents

Introduction

Raising my daughter and son is the *most* exciting, fulfilling and joyful experience of my life. Since my daughter was born seven years ago, and then my son three years later, I can honestly say that most days I wake up eager to embark on an adventure with them.

I've often said I cannot imagine how it would be to raise children in a small or even medium-sized city. A city like Chicago offers so much for families, whether it's exploring a world-class museum, taking a class at one of our first-rate and affordable local park districts or pursuing my children's latest interest such as ice skating, drumming or rock climbing. Our options are limitless.

Having said that, spending your days with children can be tedious and challenging. Some days, just getting out the door is a major feat. With this guide I hope to eliminate some of the challenges parents face—the what, where, when and how much will it cost me to raise an urban baby. Whether you are a working parent or a stay-at-home parent, *Windy City Baby* will expedite the enjoyment with your children rather than spending time researching the many options of what to do and where to go. So get out there! And enjoy everything our great city has to offer your family.

Chapter 1

Pregnancy & Childbirth

~ Hospitals—You've Got Options
~ What You Will Need for/from the Hospital
~ Obstetricians/Midwives ~ Home Birth

So you're expecting a baby! Whether you have a smooth pregnancy or a difficult one, it is certain to be one of the most remarkable times of your life. I enjoyed both of my pregnancies: I felt special and full of anticipation about becoming a mom. However, like many of you, none of my friends were pregnant when I was; in fact, I hadn't even experienced pregnancy via a friend, so everything was new to me. I had many questions but few answers, such as: how can I find a childbirth provider; should I choose an obstetrician or midwife; and, at which hospital should I deliver? Of course there is no single correct answer to any of these questions. In this chapter you will find information and resources that will help you make the best decisions for you and your family.

Hospitals—You've Got Options

In Illinois the vast majority of babies are born in hospitals. The only other option women in Illinois have is to deliver at home. Unlike many other states, Illinois does not have freestanding birth centers—homelike facilities designed according to the wellness model of pregnancy and birth, which means they approach childbirth as a natural occurrence. Fortunately, many Chicago hospitals are taking steps to make labor and delivery rooms more intimate and less institutional.

Finding the right hospital is a big decision that may affect the outcome of your birth. Many women approach childbirth with definite ideas about the type of delivery they want. For some, a desire for an unmedicated childbirth is an important goal; others may want a water birth; still others may be concerned about how mobile they can be during labor. Whatever your vision is for the birth of your child, a first step toward achieving this is selecting a hospital that can accommodate your views on childbirth. However, a reality for most of us is that we cannot choose to deliver at any hospital we wish; most of us have real limitations set by our health insurance providers. If where you deliver is important to you, start by contacting your insurance provider to find out which hospitals they are contracted with. If you have more than one hospital to choose from, then you can visit each one and select a childbirth provider who has privileges at your chosen hospital.

Below is an overview of 12 Chicago hospitals. The information is categorized so it's easier to find answers to the questions most important to you. Before you take a look at each hospital's description, review the categories below to see how and why I listed the information the way I did.

Contact Information

The contact information contains the hospital's address, phone number and Web site. Most hospitals have very detailed Web sites. You can learn a lot about the various labor and delivery programs simply by visiting the Web sites.

Visiting Hours

Every hospital I talked to allows fathers or a support person to visit 24 hours a day. Each hospital keeps separate and specific visiting hours for family and friends. Siblings must also adhere to the visitor hours unless the hospital allows them to be present at the birth.

Labor/Delivery and Postpartum Rooms

Labor and delivery rooms (LDR) and the postpartum rooms can vary greatly at hospitals. Descriptions of the basic amenities each hospital offers are detailed.

Midwives on Staff

If a hospital has midwives on staff, I indicate so.

Telemetry Monitoring

It is important to know if a hospital provides telemetry monitoring. If you are induced (given an oxytocin drip to begin labor) you will be monitored very closely, which can mean being confined to a bed during your labor. However, many hospitals offer telemetry monitoring, which allows the hospital to monitor you without limiting your mobility. This is helpful as it enables you to walk around during labor, letting gravity do some of the work.

Water Births

More and more women are choosing to deliver in water to reduce the stress and pain of childbirth. Unfortunately, few hospitals currently offer this choice. I have indicated which ones do.

Cesarean Section Rate

Cesarean section rates are once again at an all time high in America, causing alarm among many birth advocates. If you think a hospital's C-section rate is higher than you find acceptable, it pays to inquire further. Some hospitals have specific reasons for higher C-section rates. For instance, the hospital may treat a higher-risk population or have a higher percentage of multiple birth deliveries.

Nursery Level

Neonatal intensive care units are classified as levels one to three, with three being the most advanced.

Lactation Consultants

Most hospitals have lactation consultants on staff to assist you with breastfeeding. It's a good idea to meet the lactation consultant and get her phone number in case you develop problems down the road, then you will have someone to contact.

Classes

There are huge variances among the types and volume of classes the hospitals offer. I have listed current classes offered by each hospital but it always pays to call, as class schedules may change.

Hospital Listings

Advocate Illinois Masonic Medical Center
836 West Wellington Avenue   www.advocatehealth.com
773-975-1600

Visiting Hours	11:00 AM – 8:00 PM general public; 24 hours for fathers/support person.
LDR	10 suites with CD players, TVs, showers and rocking chairs. In the near future, the hospital hopes to reopen the Alternative Birthing Center, a natural childbirth center within the hospital.
Postpartum Rooms	14 rooms with TVs, showers, rocking chairs and a reclining guest chair.
Water Births	No.
Operating Rooms	Two operating rooms.
Midwives	Yes.
Telemetry Monitoring	No.
Cesarean Birthrate	23 percent.
Nursery Level	Level 3.
Lactation Consultants	Available during the day; all new moms are routinely visited by a consultant.
Classes	Gamper Childbirth Classes; a 4-week education class that uses alternative methods for childbirth. Classes focus on abdominal breathing and relaxation. Advocate also offers a nurse midwife class for patients who want to learn more about giving birth with a midwife.

Evanston Northwestern Healthcare
2650 Ridge Avenue, Evanston   www.enh.org
847-570-5020

Visiting Hours	11:00 AM – 8:30 PM general public; 24 hours for fathers/support person.
LDR	12 rooms with recliner chairs, TVs, VCRs, CD players and showers. There is one portable tub that can be brought into the room for labor but not delivery. There are four birthing balls that can also be brought into the room.
Postpartum Rooms	26 rooms plus overflow rooms with TVs, DVD and CD players, recliner

chairs, rocking chairs and whirlpools in which moms can recuperate in a sitz bath.

Water Births	No.
Operating Rooms	Two, on the same floor.
Midwives on Staff	Yes.
Telemetry Monitoring	Yes.
Cesarean Birthrate	18 percent overall; for first-time moms it's 12 percent.
Nursery Level	Level 3; also has infant special care unit where they take care of multiples.
Lactation Consultants	Available upon request every day during day hours. They also are available for phone consultations after discharge.
Classes	Extensive number of classes including Fit Beginnings Prenatal Exercise, prenatal yoga, multiples, Countdown to Labor & Delivery, Lamaze, Cesarean Birth Experience, Brothers & Sisters at Delivery, Sibling Tours, Baby Care Basics, Understanding Your Newborn, Breastfeeding Basics, Breastfeeding Growing and Nurturing, The Fourth Trimester, Expectant Grandparents, Boot Camp for New Dads, Infant & Child Safety—CPR, Car Seat Safety Class, Infant Massage and Baby & Me: Postnatal Exercise.

Lincoln Park Hospital
550 West Webster
773-883-2000

www.lincolnparkhospital.com

Visiting Hours	11:00 AM – 8:00 PM general public; 24 hours for fathers/support person.
LDR	Four rooms with showers, rocking chairs, whirlpools, pullout beds, TVs, VCRs.
Postpartum Rooms	18 rooms with guest chairs that recline, TVs, showers.
Water Births	Patients can request to deliver in the whirlpool.
Operating Rooms	One.
Midwives on Staff	Yes.
Telemetry Monitoring	Yes.
Cesarean Birthrate	32 percent.

Nursery Level	Level 2.
Lactation Consultants	No.
Classes	Basic childbirth, prenatal care, siblings class and infant massage.

Mercy Hospital and Medical Center
The Birth Place   www.mercy-chicago.org
2525 South Michigan Avenue
312-567-2441

Visiting Hours	8:00 AM – 8:00 PM general public; 24 hours for fathers/support person.
LDR	Nine rooms with showers, rocking chairs, TVs, VCRs.
Postpartum Rooms	18 rooms with fold out guest chairs, showers, TVs, and VCRs.
Water Births	No.
Operating Rooms	Three.
Midwives on Staff	Yes.
Telemetry Monitoring	No.
Cesarean Birthrate	19 percent.
Nursery Level	Level 3.
Lactation Consultants	Available upon request.
Classes	Childbirth and breastfeeding classes.

Michael Reese Hospital
2929 South Ellis
312-791-4022

Visiting Hours	1:30 PM – 9:30 PM general public; 24 hours for fathers/support person.
LDR	Eight rooms with showers, guest beds, TVs and lakefront views.
Postpartum Rooms	17 guest beds, showers, TVs and lakefront views.
Water Births	No.
Operating Rooms	Two.
Midwives on Staff	Yes.

Telemetry Monitoring	No.
Cesarean Birthrate	24 percent.
Nursery Level	Level 3.
Lactation Consultants	Available upon request.
Classes:	Childbirth classes.

Northwestern Prentice Women's Hospital
& Maternity Center
333 East Superior Street   www.nmh.org/maternity
312-926-2000

Visiting Hours	9:00 AM – 10:30 PM general public; 24 hours for fathers/support person
LDR	25 rooms with TVs, CD players, a small pull-out sofa bed, showers and refrigerators. There is also a hydro-portable labor tub and birthing balls. More women deliver at Prentice than any other hospital in Chicago. A new hospital is planned for 2007 to accommodate the growing demand.
Postpartum Rooms	The hospital has four floors of postpartum rooms, each with pullout sofa beds, showers, TVs and VCRs.
Water Births	Yes.
Operating Rooms	Three.
Midwives	Yes.
Telemetry Monitoring	Yes, in most rooms.
Cesarean Birthrate	20 percent.
Nursery Level	Level 3.
Lactation Consultants	Available upon request.
Classes	Extensive number of classes including A Baby? . . . Maybe, Baby Basics, Breastfeeding, Childbirth Education, Childbirth for Teens, Childbirth Refresher, Expectant Fathers, Expectant Grandparents, Siblings Class, Infant CPR, Infant Massage, Pediatric Care, Prenatal Exercise, Prenatal Yoga, Transitions to Motherhood, Childbirth Classes for Multiples, Breastfeeding Multiples, Parents of Multiples Club and lastly, a family birth class for parents who want their child/ren present at the labor and vaginal delivery of a sibling. Classes are available in Spanish.

Rush-Presbyterian-St. Luke's Medical Center
1650 West Harrison
312-942-5000

www.rush.edu

Visiting Hours	11:00 AM – 9:00 PM general public; 24 hours for fathers/partners.
LDR Rooms	Eight rooms with showers, TVs, rocking chairs and birthing balls.
Postpartum Rooms	16 rooms with recliner chairs that can be slept in, showers and TVs.
Water Births	No.
Operating Rooms	Two.
Midwives	Yes.
Telemetry Monitoring	Yes.
Cesarean Birthrate	34.8 percent.
Nursery Level	Level 3.
Lactation Consultants	Available during daytime hours, 7 days/week and upon request.
Classes	Birth center tour; basic breastfeeding class; Cesarean birth class; childbirth education, CPR for infants & children; marvelous multiples; refresher prenatal class; sibling class; vaginal birth after Cesarean (VBAC) class.

St. Elizabeth Hospital
Family Birthing Center
1431 North Claremont
773-278-2000

www.reshealth.org

Visiting Hours	11:00 AM – 7:00 PM general public; 24 hours for fathers/support person.
LDR Rooms	Four rooms with showers, two of the rooms have a Jacuzzi, rocking chairs, recliner lounge chairs, TVs & VCRs. Siblings can be present at birth.
Postpartum Rooms	11 Mother-Baby rooms, with recliner chairs, TVs & VCRs.
Water Births	No.
Operating Rooms	One.
Midwives	Yes.
Telemetry Monitoring	Yes.

Cesarean Birthrate	15 percent.
Nursery Level	Level 2.
Lactation Consultants	No.
Classes	Prenatal classes, parenting classes in English and Spanish, breastfeeding, infant CPR.

St Joseph Hospital
Family Birthing Unit
2900 Lake Shore Drive
773-665-3000

www.reshealth.org

Visiting Hours	10:00 AM – 8:30 PM general public; 24 hours for fathers/support person.
LDR	Eight rooms with showers, rocking chairs, refrigerators, TVs, VCRs and, best of all, real guest beds. May also have older siblings present for labor and birth.
Postpartum Rooms	28 rooms with pullout chairs that can be slept in, showers, TVs & VCRs.
Water Births	No.
Operating Rooms	Three, on the same floor.
Midwives	No.
Telemetry Monitoring	No.
Cesarean Birthrate	19 percent.
Nursery Level	Level 2.
Lactation Consultants	Yes, during the day. First-time moms are routinely visited by a consultant. Hospital provides a Breastfeeding Warmline; all calls returned within the day.
Classes	Prepared childbirth, Bradley Method, newborn care, infant/child CPR, breastfeeding and a new moms group that meets every Friday.

Swedish Covenant Family Birthing Unit
5140 North California
773-989-3834

www.schost.org

Visiting Hours	11:00 AM – 8:00 PM general public; 24 hours for fathers/support person.

LDR Rooms	Nine LDR rooms with TVs, VCRs, CD players, showers, rocking chairs, Jacuzzis, guest beds, birthing bar and birthing balls.
Postpartum Rooms	12 mother/baby recovery rooms with pullout chairs, showers, TVs, VCRs and refrigerators.
Water Births	No.
Operating Rooms	One.
Midwives	Yes.
Telemetry Monitoring	No.
Cesarean Birthrate	17 percent.
Nursery Level	Level 2.
Lactation Consultants	Yes, available every day; all new moms are routinely visited by a consultant; moms can contact consultants after discharge if needed.
Classes	Family Birthing Center Tour first Wednesday of every month; childbirth classes available in English, Hindi and Korean; & breastfeeding classes.

The University of Chicago Hospitals
5815 South Maryland Avenue   www.uchospital.edu
773-702-1000

Visiting Hours	9:00 AM – 8:00 PM general public; 24 hours a day for fathers/support person.
LDR Rooms	Ten rooms with TVs, showers, and pullout chairs.
Postpartum Rooms	13 postpartum rooms with showers, TVs, VCRs, pullout chairs and rocking chairs.
Water Births	Yes.
Operating Rooms	Four.
Midwives on Staff	No.
Telemetry Monitoring	Yes, for three beds.
Cesarean Birthrate	Unknown.
Nursery Level	Level 3.
Lactation Consultants	Yes; all new moms are routinely visited by a consultant.
Classes	The University of Chicago Hospital offers a special Childbirth

Preparation Package that includes the following classes: Beginning Breastfeeding, Infant Care for Expectant Parents, Lamaze Childbirth Preparation and a Maternity Unit Tour for $105 per couple. Expectant parents also can register for these classes independently. The Lamaze class is $90, both the breastfeeding and the infant care classes are $15 and the tour is free.

Louis A. Weiss
4646 North Marine Drive
773-564-5450

Visiting Hours	10:00 AM – 8:00 PM general public; 24 hours for fathers/support person.
LDR Rooms	11 rooms with showers, rocking chairs, guest beds, TVs and lakeside views.
Postpartum Rooms	10 postpartum rooms with fold out guest beds, showers and TVs.
Water Births	No.
Operating Rooms	Two.
Midwives on Staff	Yes.
Telemetry Monitoring	Yes.
Cesarean Birthrate	Approximately 20 percent.
Nursery Level	Level 2.
Lactation Consultants	Available upon request.
Classes	Childbirth, sibling and breastfeeding classes.

What You Will Need for/ from the Hospital

What to pack...

You'll need a lot less clothing and items at the hospital than you might think. Below is a list of what you should bring and what you can leave at home.

- You must bring an infant (rear-facing) car seat. The hospital will not discharge the baby without one.

- An adorable outfit for your new baby is a must (the hospital will give you blankets but depending on the time of year you deliver, you might want to bring one of your own).

- Of course you need a going-home outfit for yourself. This is a bit tricky. Note that I did not use the word "adorable" to describe your outfit. It is an awkward time for you. Ideally, bring a stretchy, comfortable pair of maternity pants and a top that you can breastfeed in easily.

- Do not bother bringing any of your own nightgowns because they will get messy. You may want your own robe, but hospitals offer those, too, for both walking the halls when you are in labor and for your postpartum stay.

- If you have a refrigerator in your postpartum room, then bring juice and high protein snacks. I got so tired of asking for juice after my delivery. When I did receive it, it was in those tiny cups that a woman fresh from the marathon of labor can gulp down in one swallow.

- If you are optimistic and think you will deliver your baby on the same day you go into labor, then bring the day's newspaper because many nurses will put your baby's footprints on the headline of the day's paper—a nice keepsake. Along those same lines, bring your baby book and ask the nurse to put your baby's precious footprints in it.

- If you are picky about your pillows, then bring one from home, but understand that things can get messy. After your child's birth you will only have eyes for her/him and you might forget it when you are transferred to a postpartum room.

- You should have your insurance information, though it pays to preregister at the hospital when you go for a tour or childbirth classes.

- You may bring your cell phone but many hospitals will not allow you to have it turned on in the hospital as it can interfere with hospital equipment. However, after your baby is born your partner can always go outside to use the phone and spread the good news.

- Breath mints can be helpful during labor (this is my husband's suggestion!). During both of my labors I was not allowed to drink or eat anything. One's breath can get a bit unpleasant when you are working hard and not taking in fluids, so bring a mint. It is surprisingly refreshing when that is all you've got.

- You need your own toiletries... toothbrush/toothpaste, contacts, glasses, lotion, shampoo/conditioner, whatever it takes to make you feel fresh and beautiful!

- Music! If your hospital has a CD player (you could always bring your own) you may want to use music to ease the stress of labor. Here's a project for your partner—have him create a special labor-day CD for your big event.

- Of course you will want your camera to photograph your beautiful new baby and maybe the labor too. Some people also choose to videotape their labor and birth. If you wish to do this, check with the hospital because hospitals may have specific rules as to what and when you can videotape.

Now for the really important list... What you take from the hospital

The items that hospitals offer new moms vary, but there are staples that you should make sure not to pass up.

- Hospitals have these wonderful, disposable icepacks that feel so good on your very sore bottom. I used them for my entire postpartum stay. Medical professionals will tell you that the ice only helps the swelling for 24 hours but if you have a tear or had an episiotomy ice can help numb the pain long after those first 24 hours. Ask for as many as they will give you and sit on them off-and-on once you get home.

- Hospitals also have ingenious small heating packs that heat up when you crush them in your hands. These heating packs can help get your milk to flow before your baby latches onto your breast.

- Take the "chux" with you. These are absorbent, disposable paper pads that you sit or lie on for a while after giving birth to protect the linens. Most postpartum women experience a lot of bleeding for a week or two (or longer) after giving birth. Why ruin all your sheets and furniture? Ask the nurse for as many of these as she will give you.

- Some hospitals will give you receiving blankets, diapers and the cute crossover t-shirts. Take them—you will need many of these.

- Many hospitals give you booklets or informational sheets on newborn care, breastfeeding, postpartum care and more. Often these handouts have invaluable information that is easier and faster to read than baby books. Also, these handouts have helpful phone numbers of services you can seek for any number of issues from postpartum depression, to breastfeeding, to emergency pediatric care. Use these handouts to build your parenting library.

Home Birth—An alternative to birthing in a hospital

Homefirst
Lincoln Park Hospital
550 West Webster Place
773-883-3890
Other locations throughout Chicago

www.homefirst.com

Some women find a home birth their best option. If you desire an intimate birthing environment, free of medical interventions, then you may want to investigate having a home birth. You don't have to be an avid reader of *People* magazine to know that many celebrities are choosing to have their babies at home. Maybe you'd like to join the ranks of Cindy Crawford, Julianne Moore and Kelly Preston and try a home birth. If so, you'll want to contact Homefirst.

Homefirst has five prenatal offices and is affiliated with several area hospitals including Swedish Covenant, Norwegian American and Lincoln Park Hospitals. Its practice consists of physicians and certified nurse-midwives specially trained to provide you and your baby with a safe home birth experience.

Homefirst has delivered more than 15,000 babies at home in the metropolitan Chicago area. Homefirst hosts frequent home birth seminars so that moms-to-be and their partners can learn more about this safe, intimate and increasingly popular way of welcoming your baby into the world.

Home Birth & Women's Health, Inc.
400 East 22nd Street, Suite F
Lombard
708-445-8206

www.homebirthandwomenshealth.com

Home Birth & Women's Health Inc. is a practice of certified nurse-midwives who provide home birth services. They approach childbirth as a natural and healthy event in a woman's life. Women who are experiencing a low-risk pregnancy are capable of delivering at home. A woman that has had a previous C-section, is carrying twins or whose baby is breech cannot deliver at home. The practice accepts medical insurance. Back-up physicians are on call in the event that the patient cannot deliver at home. Free consultations are available.

Obstetricians/Midwives

Finding the right caregiver for your pregnancy and labor is the most important decision you will make during your pregnancy. When choosing between an obstetrician and a midwife, you and your partner have many things to consider, such as:

- What type of birth experience do you want to have?
- Do you have any known risk factors that may lead to complications in your pregnancy or the birth of your baby?
- Do you want a provider who is part of a group practice?
- What is your approach to childbirth – do you want an unmedicated childbirth; are there specific pain medications and interventions that you want or wish to avoid?
- Is there a certain hospital you would prefer for your delivery?
- What restrictions does your insurance provider place on you?
- How much support do you want during labor?

Obstetricians

In Chicago, as in most of America, obstetricians deliver the majority of babies. You most likely already have an obstetrician/gynecologist (ob/gyn) and now must decide if you want your current physician to deliver your baby. Even if you are happy with your current ob/gyn being pregnant is a very different experience than going for annual checkups. Take this opportunity to ask yourself and your ob/gyn some questions to make sure you are a good match.

If you decide to find a new ob/gyn for your pregnancy you can begin by asking friends with children if they would recommend their obstetrician. Also, the American College of Obstetrician and Gynecologist has a Web site that you can search to find a local physician. Visit their Web site at www.acog.com and click on "find a physician."

To learn if your childbirth philosophy is the same as your physician's you can begin by asking the following questions:

- What is the average length of an appointment and how often are appointments scheduled?
- Which tests does your physician recommend for everyone and which tests require a more individualized decision?

- What are your physician's views on episiotomy, pain medication, labor induction, unmedicated childbirth, use of a doula during delivery, and breastfeeding?
- Is the physician part of a group practice? If so, will you visit all the physicians in the practice during your pregnancy? If the physician is part of a group practice who will deliver your baby?
- What is the physician's Cesarean section rate?
- With which hospital(s) is the physician affiliated?
- What is the process for answering your questions between appointments?
- Which insurance plans does the physician accept? Does she or he offer payment plans for expenses not covered by insurance?
- Is your pregnancy considered high-risk?

Midwives

Worldwide, most babies are delivered by midwives and it is increasingly a more popular choice in America, with midwives delivering approximately 9 percent of all births in the United States, an increase of 100 percent from 1990 to 2001. Many of my friends have chosen to use a midwife because of the more personalized and attentive care midwives can provide. For example, the practice of many widwives is to be with you throughout your labor and birth.

A certified nurse midwife has been trained in two disciplines: midwifery and nursing, and must be accredited by the American College of Nurse Midwives. Certified nurse-midwives are able to administer drugs, perform medical procedures and provide their patients with other technological interventions, if desired. During labor, midwives can prescribe pain medication and call an anesthesiologist should you request an epidural.

As is true with many physicians, a midwife's approach to your pregnancy extends beyond the birth experience to include prenatal care, nutrition, breastfeeding, infant care and the emotional aspects of your pregnancy. A midwife also can offer the mother postpartum care in the form of support and information regarding the physical and emotional changes the mother is experiencing. According to a 1997 study in the *American Journal of Public Health*, women working with certified nurse-midwives underwent fewer medical birth interventions, such as episiotomies and Cesarean sections, than those attended by obstetricians and family physicians. However, it's important to note that midwives do not typically take care of higher risk patients. This may be one reason why physicians perform more medical interventions.

To find a certified nurse midwife go to the American College of Nurse Midwives Web site at acnm.org and click on "find midwife."

Chicago Community Midwives
847-658-2318   www.chicagocommunitymidwives.org

Chicago Community Midwives provides education and advocacy. It conducts both community and professional education. If you are considering a midwife for your delivery or are looking for a referral, call this organization.

Chapter 2

Preparing for the Big Day

~ Childbirth Education ~ Childbirth Classes ~ Doulas ~ Prenatal Massage
~ Prenatal/Postnatal Exercise ~ Breastfeeding Support
~ Infant Massage

Now that you've selected a childbirth provider and a hospital there is still plenty to do to help ensure a healthy pregnancy and the childbirth experience you want. It's time to educate your mind and tend to your growing body—in short, prepare for your big day.

Childbirth Education

Most hospitals offer childbirth classes, which can be a great way to prepare for your delivery and an opportunity to familiarize yourself with your hospital (see previous chapter). However, you are certainly not limited to the classes your hospital offers. There are many unique programs available to you and your partner. For example, you can explore hypnosis during birth, the Bradley childbirth method, or the Lamaze method, and learn more about alternatives to medications and the hospital tradition of delivering on your back.

BirthLink
1555 Sherman Street   www.birthlink.com
Evanston
847-733-8050

BirthLink is a great place to research your many childbirth options. Founder Jo Anne Lindberg has created a phenomenal resource for both parents-to-be and parents, including information on physicians, midwives, doulas, childbirth educators, massage therapists, parenting classes, new moms groups, prenatal yoga, breastfeeding and much more. Lindberg is an advocate for nonintervention childbirth, breastfeeding and infant bonding. BirthLink offers educational programs but you also can learn a lot just by visiting the Web site.

Below is a description of some of the various childbirth methods you may wish to explore.

Association of Labor Assistants & Childbirth Educators (ALACE)   www.alace.org

ALACE childbirth educators approach childbirth as a woman-centered and woman-directed passage, not an institution-centered medical event. ALACE childbirth educators teach relaxation and coping tools to work with pain and discomfort, rather than "techniques" for avoiding sensation. Visit their Web site to find ALACE educators in your area.

The Bradley Method   www.bradleybirth.com

The Bradley Method teaches natural childbirth and views birth as a natural process. Women are encouraged to use breathing, relaxation and the support of a "coach" (partner or husband) to give birth naturally. Visit the above Web site to find a convenient class in your area.

HypnoBirthing   www.hypnobirthing.com

HypnoBirthing is a method that is gaining popularity in which the laboring woman uses learned techniques to relax so that her body's natural birthing instincts can take over for a calm birth experience. Laboring women using the HypnoBirthing technique are not in a trance or asleep but rather in a state of deep, calm focus that allows the body's natural anesthesia, called endorphins, to replace the stress hormones that cause pain. Visit the above Web site to find an instructor in your area.

Lamaze International   www.lamaze.org

The Lamaze method believes that childbirth is a normal, natural and healthy experience that women can go through without medical intervention. Lamaze also believes that the experience of birth profoundly affects women and their families. Lamaze uses breathing techniques (the ones you see comically imitated by laboring women on television) to work with contractions. Visit the above Web site for an instructor in your area.

Childbirth Classes

Listed below are childbirth classes that you may wish to pursue as an alternative to or in addition to the class(es) offered at the hospital where you will deliver. Some of these educators employ the various methods described above.

Birthways, Inc.
1473 West Farragut   www.birthwaysinc.com
773-506-0607

Birthways offers group childbirth classes that provide thorough information about what to expect from prenatal care, the labor process, the birthing environment (hospital or home) and your relationship with your care provider, whether she/he be an obstetrician or midwife. Birthways also offers in-home childbirth education. In addition to childbirth classes, it provides in-home breastfeeding classes, infant CPR, baby sign language, understanding your baby and other classes. Classes are $25 per person or $40 per couple.

ChildBearing Gifts
650 North Dearborn, Suite 200   www.childbearinggifts.com
312-446-9296

Pam Bogda, a registered nurse with more than 20 years of experience in maternal-child nursing, makes her expertise available to expectant parents through her business, ChildBearing Gifts. Pam offers a comprehensive childbirth education class that includes information on natural childbirth, the Bradley Method, the Lamaze breathing technique, pain medication options and more. The class is offered in a 4-week session or an intensive one-day session for $115 per couple. Pam also teaches a one-time breastfeeding class that is offered twice monthly for $65 and an infant CPR class for $25. There is also a prenatal yoga class (see prenatal exercise section in this chapter). Pregnant moms will love "The Divine Comfort Bag." It is an exquisite bag loaded with comfort products for pregnant and/or laboring women. The bag is $99 and includes her childbirth comfort book and CD, massage tools, a microwaveable heat pad, lavender massage cream and the all-important lip balm for a laboring woman whose fluid intake is restricted.

Deanne Falzone
773-278-8382   www.knowyourbirth.com

Deanne Falzone is a Bradley childbirth educator offering weekly classes in the Ukranian Village neighborhood. A 12-week session is $275.

Mary Flores

773-735-0114   maryflores@redjellyfish.net

Mary Flores, a Bradley childbirth educator since 2002, teaches classes on the southwest side of Chicago. A 12-week session is $275.

Diana Germany

312-735-0730   rjg@uchicago.edu

Diana Germany, a Bradley childbirth educator since 2002, teaches classes in Hyde Park. A 10-week session is $275.

Therese Hawks R.N., BSN, CH

773-506-6318   www.hypnobirthingchicago.net

For the past three years Therese Hawks has taught HypnoBirthing, a process in which moms-to-be and their partners use relaxation and self-hypnosis techniques to eliminate the fear, tension and, yes, pain of labor and replace it with an easier, peaceful, more comfortable labor. Sounds good, doesn't it? This process is taught in four, 2-1/2 hour classes or over two Saturdays. The price ranges from $275–$350 and includes the classes, two tapes and a book.

Labor Positions and Childbirth Support

Global Yoga   www.globalyogacenter.com
1823 West North Avenue
773-489-1510

This class is for couples in the third trimester of pregnancy. Instructor Rhonda Kantor has more than 11 years of nursing experience and is a nationally certified holistic nurse through the American Holistic Nursing Association. Rhonda leads a two-hour workshop to help prepare couples for the birth experience. Couples have the opportunity to practice comfort positions for labor, birth positions, yoga poses, abdominal breathing, partner support and relaxation techniques. Rhonda offers this workshop once a month for a fee of $40 per couple.

Mama Belly Birth Services

Sweet Pea's Studio   www.mamabellybirth.com
3717 North Ravenswood   www.alace.org
773-465-4337

Instructor Natalie Evans is an ALACE (Association of Labor Assistants and Child Birth Educators) childbirth educator. Evans' philosophy is "restoring women's confidence, strength and joy in childbearing." The classes are natural childbirth classes. Group classes are $200 for a 7-week session or private classes are $70 for a 3-hour session.

Starbaby

Childbirth and Parenting Education   www.starbabybirthandparenting.com
"Awaiting the Child: Pregnancy, Labor and Birth"

Christine Culbert, RN, BSN, CCE (ALACE)
773-381-9728

Starbaby is a 7-week class for expectant parents in which Christine provides an overview of birth in our culture, birthing options, comfort measures, decision-making when labor is not going as desired, information on welcoming your baby and understanding the newborn experience. Christine fully comprehends and respects the wonder of pregnancy and childbirth. Her prenatal and parent/baby classes (see Chapter 3) help ignite the love affair between new parents and their baby. The 7-week class is $200; private instruction also is available.

Sweet Pea's Studio
Jennifer Barron Fishman, Director,
& Corinne Peterson, Associate Director
3717 North Ravenswood, Suite 213
773-248-YOGA

www.sweetpeasstudio.com

Sweet Pea's Studio is a fabulous resource for parents and parents-to-be. A variety of classes and workshops are offered, which include "Comfort Measures for Childbirth"—a 7-week childbirth preparation class, breastfeeding workshops, prenatal yoga, prenatal partners' yoga, baby and me yoga, and other specialized workshops such as, acupressure, hypnosis and visualization. Sweet Pea's also has three massage therapists on staff specializing in prenatal and postpartum massage. This studio offers so many rich classes that the best thing to do is go to their Web site for detailed information and a schedule.

Doulas

A doula is a professionally trained person who helps families during and after childbirth. That assistance can come in many forms—from helping laboring women make decisions during the childbirth process to offering comfort and massage to ease the pain of labor to advocating for the laboring woman and her family during the birth process. I had a doula for my second childbirth and I have no doubt that she is the reason I was able to have a vaginal birth after my first C-section.

Every laboring woman and her family can benefit from having a doula. Let's face it, most of us are amateurs at this childbirth thing and to expect our partners to know what we need and when we need it may be setting expectations too high. During both of my 24 hour labors my husband became extremely tired and even napped a bit. I was a little ticked off about that during my first labor, but with my second one I had a doula helping me so I actually wanted him to rest so he would be ready for my pushing marathon. It was a different experience and a better outcome for both my husband and me!

A doula also can be hired to help *after* your baby is born, which is another great option. A postpartum doula offers support to the recuperating mother, answers questions about baby care and breastfeeding, and may even make meals, do laundry and run errands so that mom and the new family can focus only on their bundle of joy.

For general information about doulas and for referrals, go to the Doulas of North America's Web site at www.dona.org. I have included below a list of incredible doula services.

"A Mother Is Born" Postpartum Doula Services
Peggy Healy, MS
6214 North Normandy Avenue
773-774-9705

Peggy, who has five children of her own, is a postpartum doula and a student lactation consultant with a master's degree in counseling. Peggy's goal is to provide the support necessary to make the postpartum period positive and rewarding for the whole family. She accomplishes this by helping the mother with her physical and emotional recovery from childbirth, assisting with breastfeeding and newborn care and helping with all the necessities such as meal preparation, errands, sibling care, light laundry and housekeeping. Peggy charges by the hour.

Birthways, Inc.
1484 West Farragut   www.birthwaysinc.com
773-506-0607

Birthways, Inc. is an excellent resource for both labor and postpartum doulas. Birthways' doulas have a great reputation among moms; they are trained by, and members of, the Association of Labor Assistants and Childbirth Educators or Doulas of North America. Birthways' doulas receive professional training in postpartum care and continuing education throughout the year. Many of their doulas have additional certifications or licensure in fields related to childbearing and healthcare. A labor support doula is available for $700, which includes as much prenatal time as desired, the entire labor and a postpartum follow-up visit. A sliding scale fee is available.

Birthways postpartum doulas provide a new mom and her family with resources, answer all your new-parent questions and take such good care of you and your family that the first few weeks can be the joyful honeymoon with your baby that it should be. Postpartum doulas help with newborn care, breastfeeding support, meal preparation, shopping or other errands, laundry, light housekeeping and sibling care. Postpartum doulas are available at a rate of $25/hour for the first 50 hours and $23/hour after 50 hours. A four-hour minimum per day is required.

Blooming Iris Birth Companions
Susan Gallas CD, CBM   bloomingiris@hotmail.com
847-949-4249

Susan Gallas is a labor and postpartum doula since 1999. Her labor support service includes two to three prenatal visits (including one physician/midwife visit), the labor and birth and two to eight hours of postpartum care. Her fee for labor support ranges from $875 to $1000, depending on the level of postpartum care required. Susan is also a postpartum doula specializing in multiples birth care. She provides total family care and charges by the hour; $25 to $40 depending on the size of the family.

Creating Balance
Elizabeth Nostvick   www.creatingbalancemt.com
3354 North Paulina
773-758-0607

For more than four years Elizabeth Nostvick has worked with both pregnant women and postpartum moms to provide a variety of services including pre/postnatal massage, pre/postnatal exercise and postpartum support. As a postpartum doula, Elizabeth provides care for the new mom, assistance with breastfeeding, newborn care and help with food or housekeeping support. Elizabeth is affiliated with Birthways, Inc.

Abigail Lynn, CMT
773-991-7968   abidoula@aol.com

Abigail Lynn is a birth doula whose philosophy is that women can deliver naturally though she is supportive of the couple's choices for the birth or their child. As part of her service she meets with the couple for two prenatal visits, which includes a mini-massage for mom-to-be. She is with the laboring woman for as long as she wants during delivery and then does one postnatal visit during which she teaches the new parents how to do infant massage. A doula for four years, her service is available for a flat rate of $700. She also provides in-home pre and postnatal massage for $80 an hour and $110 for an hour and a half.

Mama Belly Birth Services
Natalie Evans   mamabellybirth.com
773-465-4337

Natalie Evans is a doula, DONA-trained (Doulas of North America) and a birth educator. She has attended a wide variety of births in the home and hospital settings, including VBAC and Cesarean births.

Right from the Start, Postpartum Doula Services
Ellen McManus   emm@voyager.net
847-251-3778

Ellen McManus has more than 20 years of experience with maternal and child care. She is an instructor and consultant at Prentice Women's Hospital and conducts breastfeeding classes in corporate settings. Ellen is certified in lactation, childbirth education, infant massage and as a postpartum doula. As a postpartum doula she can provide lactation support and education, emotional support, newborn care, postpartum care for mom, infant massage and light housekeeping. In addition to her wealth of professional experience, she is the mother of a special needs child and an adopted child whom she nursed. In short, there is probably no situation that she has not encountered with her breadth of experience. Fees are individually set according to the family's needs.

Rhonda Kantor
Global Yoga and Wellness Center
1823 West North Avenue
773-489-1510

Rhonda Kantor has a fantastic breadth of experience to help you with your labor and childbirth. Rhonda encourages women to make their own childbirth choices based on information from both the medical and alternative care model. In addition to being a doula, Rhonda is a registered nurse, a certified holistic nurse and a registered yoga teacher. Her services are available for $600.

Prenatal Massage

Massage during pregnancy is a wonderful way to alleviate the many stresses your body experiences. Most massage therapists request that you check with your midwife or physician before having a massage. Many of the women listed in the doula section also provide prenatal massage so refer back to that section too.

Birthways, Inc.
1473 West Farragut   www.birthwaysinc.com
773-506-0607

Birthways is known for excellent prenatal and postnatal education and doula services, and also offers in-home and in-studio massage.

Blooming Bellies
Melissa Marcoux   www.bloomingbellies.com
Prenatal & postnatal massage
1344 North Milwaukee Avenue, 3rd Floor
773-269-2877

At Blooming Bellies you will not find a table with a belly hole because it can add strain to an already stressed lower back; instead Melissa puts moms-to-be in side-lying and semi-reclined seated positions, completely supported by pillows—it's like being massaged on a cloud! In addition to prenatal and postnatal massage Melissa will show the mom-to-be some "tricks" to help ease the discomforts of pregnancy and labor. Melissa conducts an intake evaluation to see how the mom-to-be is feeling before each session and to tailor the massage session to her particular needs. Sessions are 30 minutes ($40), one hour ($70) or 90 minutes ($100).

Corinne Peterson, MPH
Sweet Pea's Studio   www.sweetpeasstudio.com
3717 North Ravenswood, Suite 213
773-562-5933

Corrine is a massage therapist, prenatal/postpartum yoga instructor and childbirth educator. She also is a birth doula, working on a limited basis at the present time, primarily with families she's worked with previously. As a massage therapist she offers prenatal and postpartum massage including, "Bouncing Back from Baby," an in-depth postpartum massage series. Massages are $75 per hour.

Creating Balance
Elizabeth Nostvick   www.creatingbalancemt.com
3354 North Paulina
773-758-0607

For more than four years Elizabeth Nostvick has worked with both pregnant women and postpartum moms to provide a variety of services that include pre/postnatal massage, pre/postnatal exercise and postpartum doula work. An in-studio massage is $70 for one hour, $100 for 90 minutes. In home massages are $100 for one hour and $130 for 90 minutes.

Global Yoga and Wellness Center
1823 West North Avenue   www.globalyogacenter.com
773-489-1510

Rhonda Kantor, childbirth educator, doula and prenatal/postnatal yoga instructor also offers prenatal massage for $70 per hour.

Jennifer Barron Fishman
Sweet Pea's Studio   www.sweetpeasstudio.com
3717 North Ravenswood, Suite 213
773-248-YOGA

Jennifer is a massage therapist specializing in bodywork for the childbearing year. She offers a program called "Bouncing Back from Baby," and infant massage. An additional benefit to working with Jennifer is that she is a trained labor support and postpartum doula. Jennifer approaches pregnancy and childbirth as the amazing time in one's life that it is and aims to instill in women confidence in themselves and their bodies. She also helps educate and inform women and their families about their many choices during pregnancy and childbirth. Massages are $75 per hour.

Prenatal/Postnatal Exercise

Exercise during pregnancy is a great way to manage the aches and discomforts that can accompany pregnancy, revel in your changing body and/or to simply, relax. Any exercise program you select will ask you to first obtain permission from your ob/gyn or midwife before participating in a class. Also, look for an instructor who is certified in pre and postnatal exercise. Listed below are some great programs to check out.

ChildBearing Gifts
650 North Dearborn, Suite 200   www.childbrearinggifts.com
312-446-9296

In addition to the great educational classes that ChildBearing Gifts offers, it also hosts a weekly prenatal yoga class. The class meets every week and is $15 per class or $65 for five classes.

The Galter Life Center
5157 North Francisco Avenue   www.galterlifecenter.org
773-878-9936

The Galter Life Center is a great health club that provides 8- or 9-week sessions in prenatal yoga and prenatal strength and stamina. The instructors are certified in prenatal and postnatal instruction. Classes are offered once or twice weekly. A session cost is $90 for non-members and $70 for members. If participants take two classes a week they can do so at a reduced rate. The Galter Center also has plans to add a baby & me class and an exercise class for moms with mobile kids, possibly a stroller class. Contact Leslie for details. The Galter Life Center has a free parking lot.

Global Yoga and Wellness Center
1823 West North Avenue   www.globalyogacenter.com
773-489-1510

Global Yoga offers yoga classes for both prenatal and postnatal women. "Prenatal Hatha Yoga" is a safe and gentle approach for women in each stage of pregnancy. This class focuses on body alignment, breathing exercises and strengthening for the mind, body and spirit. This class is excellent preparation for birth as it promotes concentration, relaxation and flexibility. In the "Mom & Baby Yoga Class" the focus is on restorative and strengthening for new moms. New moms can bring along their babies up until their first birthday. Classes are $12 each or eight classes for $85.

Lakeshore Athletic Club

Lincoln Park location
1320 West Fullerton
773-477-9888

www.lsac.com

This athletic club has a highly specialized program called "The Fit Mom's Club," which offers a variety of classes including water and studio classes. The classes are designed so that moms-to-be can get to know one another. For the postnatal mom, Lakeshore offers "Baby Boot Camp & Sculpt," which includes stroller classes and mom-n-baby yoga. Babies can come to class or go to the nursery (babies are accepted beginning at six weeks). All instructors are pre- and postnatal certified. Punch cards are available for purchase. Five classes for $93, 10 classes for $151and 20 classes for $232.

Lincoln Park Athletic Club

1019 West Diversey
773-529-2022

www.lpaconline.com

Lincoln Park Athletic Club offers pre and postnatal exercise classes, water workouts and yoga for both members and non-members. To participate in these programs, non-members can purchase a 10-visit pass for $150 or a 20-visit pass for $240.

Northwestern Prentice Women's Hospital & Maternity Center

333 East Superior Street
312-926-2000

www.nmh.org/maternity

Northwestern Prentice Women's Hospital & Maternity Center offers several exercise programs for both prenatal and postpartum moms. The options include prenatal aerobics, yoga, prenatal Nia and postnatal body sculpting.

Sweet Pea's Studio

3717 North Ravenswood, Suite 213
773-248-YOGA

www.sweetpeasstudio.com

Sweet Pea's offers prenatal yoga and baby-and-me yoga classes. Yoga is an excellent way to prepare the body for all of the changes it goes through during pregnancy. Yoga teaches strength and stamina as well as concentration and breath control, both of which are invaluable tools during labor and birth. In addition, Sweet Pea's Studio has yoga classes for new moms to help with postpartum recovery. A one-hour class is available for $13 for drop-in or $11 per class for an 8-week session. Ninety-minute classes are $15 for drop-in or $13 per class for an 8-week session.

Walk-A-Bye Baby

773-244-8020

www.walkabyebaby.com

Walk-A-Bye Baby is a fun, energizing approach to both prenatal and postnatal exercise. It has "stroller classes" held in Lincoln Park, or indoors in bad weather at Windy City Fitness, toning classes for moms only (a sitter watches the children), mom-and-baby yoga and prenatal classes. The prenatal classes focus on cardio, strengthening and specific childbirth and recovery exercises, such as breathing, abdominal and strengthening kegels. Walk-A-Bye Baby is a great way to get out with your new baby and meet other new moms. All classes are taught by certified prenatal/postnatal fitness instructors and meet American College of Obstetricians and Gynecologist guidelines. A 12-week session costs $175–$185 depending on the specific class.

Breastfeeding Support

Breast milk is the perfect food for your baby with components that cannot be duplicated by formula. Breastfeeding also is an incredibly loving and nurturing act, creating a wonderful bond between mom and baby. There are numerous health benefits for mom and baby. For instance, breastfeeding can boost your baby's immune system and studies are now showing it can also increase your child's IQ, reduce childhood obesity and possibly reduce your baby's chance of developing certain cancers. In fact, the American Academy of Pediatrics recommends that babies are exclusively breastfed for the first six months and continue to breastfeed for the first year of life. However, some women find breastfeeding to be harder than it looks—but usually only at first.

When my daughter was born I had a difficult time breastfeeding, to the point that she lost more than 20 percent of her birth weight and my milk supply dwindled. However, I was committed to breastfeeding and fortunately my daughter's pediatrician recommended a lactation consultant. A lactation consultant can make all the difference in the world! My lactation consultant promptly came to my home, worked with me on positioning and technique, helped me obtain the necessary equipment to increase my milk supply and most importantly, gave me the confidence to breastfeed.

The reality is that most of today's new moms were not breastfed as babies, which means that most new grandmas cannot offer much help when it comes to learning this skill in a baby's vital first week of life. It is therefore imperative that you prepare yourself: take the breastfeeding classes, read the books, ask to see a lactation consultant before you leave the hospital and do not hesitate to request a lactation consultant to come to your home!

Below is a list of wonderful lactation consultants. You also can find a lactation consultant by contacting your baby's pediatrician or your obstetrician or midwife.

Art of Breastfeeding, Inc.

Cynthia Guzman, IBCLC, RLC   www.artofbreastfeeding.com
773-745-0992

Cynthia Guzman is an International Board Certified Lactation Consultant in private practice. She conducts in-home consultations, which include assistance with technique, recommendations for equipment rentals/purchases and most importantly, demonstrations on how to use breast pumps or any other breastfeeding equipment desired by the mom. Her fee is $175 and includes as much follow-up care or consultations as necessary. Cynthia also gives new moms the necessary billing information to submit to their insurance provider for reimbursement.

Breast 'N Baby Lactation Services, Inc.

Carol Chamblin   www.breastbabyproducts.com
630-513-1101

Carol offers a great service for new moms committed to breastfeeding. For a one-time fee of $190, Carol includes a prenatal visit in which she educates the soon-to-be-mom about breastfeeding, meets her at the hospital after delivery to help with breastfeeding and any other issues, and visits the new mom in her home a few days after birth (once the mom's milk has come in) to ensure that breastfeeding is going smoothly. In addition, Carol sells or rents pumps, provides instruction on how to use pumps, conducts prenatal breastfeeding classes, teaches infant massage and runs support groups. Carol also gives new moms the necessary billing information to submit to their insurance provider for reimbursement.

Ellen McManus, LE

847-251-3778   emm@voyager.net

For more than 20 years, Ellen has helped new moms breastfeed their babies. Ellen provides private in-home consultations and teaches breastfeeding classes at Northwestern Memorial's Prentice Hospital and for private corporations. As a certified lactation consultant, Ellen has experience working with adoptive mothers who want to breastfeed and with mothers who want to breastfeed children with special needs. Ellen also is a doula and teaches a variety of classes, including infant massage, transitions into motherhood and a grandparent's class.

The Mother's Milk Company

Barbara Hardin
708-652-0060

Lactation consultant Barbara Hardin helps new moms succeed at breastfeeding. For a one-time fee of $185 Barbara comes to your home and helps with any breastfeeding questions or struggles. She provides on-going phone consultations after the initial home visit for no additional fee. Barbara also gives new moms the necessary billing information to submit to their insurance provider for reimbursement.

Your Breastfeeding Rights

The Illinois Right to Breastfeed Act guarantees "a mother may breastfeed her baby in any location, public or private, where the mother is otherwise authorized to be." So whether you are at a pool, store or restaurant your right to breastfeed you baby is protected.

Infant Massage

Many parents praise the benefits of infant massage, which can provide health benefits for your baby and can be a great bonding experience for mom or dad and baby.

Chicago Area Certified Infant Massage Instructors
847-289-4563   www.infantmassageinstructors.com

Finding a certified infant massage instructor is important to learning the proper technique. The Chicago Area Certified Infant Massage Instructors can give you the names and contact information of certified instructors in your area.

Ellen McManus, LE
847-251-3778   emm@voyager.net

Ellen teaches infant massage in addition to her many other skills as a lactation consultant, childbirth educator and doula.

Sweet Pea's Studio
Jennifer Barron Fishman,   www.sweetpeasstudio.com
Director, & Corinne Peterson, Associate Director
3717 North Ravenswood, Suite 213
773-248-YOGA

Sweet Pea offers "Infant Massage Classes," which provide personal instruction on how to massage your baby.

Chapter 3

Welcome to the Parenthood Club

~ Community Organizations & Services ~ Parent & Baby's First Class
~ Hotlines ~ Help in the Kitchen! ~ Support Groups

One of the best parts about becoming a parent is the instant kinship you can find with other parents. It happens at the local Starbucks when you and another weary-eyed parent strike up a conversation about your baby's sleep habits while awaiting your lattes. It happens in the grocery store when your baby erupts with cries because she's decided now is the perfect moment to breastfeed, and another parent exchanges a knowing look and sympathetic words. However, in a city the size of Chicago you do not have to wait for these serendipitous moments. You can seek out just about any support and community group to fit your family's needs. In this chapter you will find information about support groups, new parent groups, hotlines and more.

Community Organizations & Services

There are many organizations and support groups available to you and your new baby. These groups vary in terms of programming, but what they all have in common is the desire to help nurture you as a parent and enrich your family life. Below are descriptions of great organizations that you will enjoy getting to know.

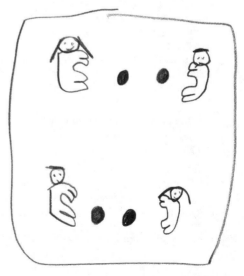

BabyMe

211 East Ohio Street, Suite 1001 www.baby-me.net
312-222-9770

Grace Diegel and Karyn Lasin have created an inspired and valuable service through BabyMe. Both Grace and Karyn are postpartum nurses who strive to help new families with the transition from the hospital to home. Their services include essential newborn care, breastfeeding assistance, nursery organization, circumcision care, infant CPR and more. In addition to the specific information and skills Grace and Karyn share, their ultimate goal is to promote the parent's confidence because they believe that parents know best! BabyMe is a perfect new baby gift from out-of-town grandparents. The gift certificate is "wrapped" in a cloth diaper and secured with a ducky safety pin—adorable. Call for fee information.

Birthways, Inc.

1473 West Farragut www.birthwaysinc.com
773-506-0607

Whether or not you got to know Birthways when you were pregnant you will want to know them once your baby is born. Birthways creates a very family-friendly atmosphere and offers family classes including infant CPR, baby sign language, understanding your baby and more. Classes are $25 per person or $40 for a couple.

Fussy Baby Network

Erikson Institute www.erikson.edu
420 North Wabash, 3rd Floor
888-431-BABY

The Fussy Baby Network is a unique program created in 2003 by the Erikson Institute, a renowned graduate program in early childhood education. This program is available to any parent who would like help in dealing with a "fussy" baby. The Institute can provide assistance over the phone or conduct home visits, if desired. Through a partnership with the University of Chicago, it has on staff a pediatrician, an occupational therapist and a psychiatrist. The network is a host to parent groups and in-services regarding breastfeeding and infant massage. The network provides its services on a sliding scale fee, based on income, and offers in-home visits for free or up to $50.

Hyde Park Neighborhood Club

5480 South Kenwood Avenue www.hpnclub.org
773-643-4062

The Hyde Park Neighborhood Club is a great resource for Hyde Park parents. One of the club's best programs is the "Tot Lot," an indoor play program for babies through four year olds and their parents/caregivers. From October through May the Hyde Park Neighborhood Club opens its gymnasium three mornings a week so that toddlers can ride big wheels, play on climbing toys and run around while parents/caregivers connect. At only $150 for the year, it's a real lifesaver for families enduring another long Chicago winter. The club offers dance programs, piano, biddy-basketball and t-ball. For school age children the club runs both before and after school programs, offering arts-and-crafts, indoor and outdoor play and help with homework. There is also a park, Nichols Park, behind the building.

Hyde Park Parent Support Network

http://groups.yahoo.com/group/parentssupportgroup
(located in the First Unitarian Church)
5650 South Woodlawn Avenue

The Hyde Park Parent Support Network is an informal organization of approximately 100 families. The group runs a "playroom" four mornings a week at the First Unitarian Church (except for the summer months). The parent network also operates an e-mail listserve for members to chat about parenting and/or community issues. Finally, it issues a newsletter approximately four times a year. The best way to get in touch with this group is either to stop by the church or write to the above e-mail address. The Hyde Park Parent Support Network is an all-volunteer organization and relies on membership fees to function. It suggests an annual membership fee of $75, but no family will be turned away.

La Leche League International

800-525-3243   www.lalecheleague.org

Since 1956, La Leche League has been the biggest advocate and supporter of mothers who want to breastfeed their babies. Originally started by a group of moms, La Leche League is now an international not-for-profit organization. Even if you do not have any questions or problems with breastfeeding La Leche is a great community of support. La Leche League groups meet monthly in several locations throughout Chicago. See its Web site for locations. If you need immediate help, call the hotline to locate a La Leche League leader in your area to help you through any breastfeeding struggles.

The Mother-Infant Connection

The Family and Child Development Center of the Juvenile Protection Agency
1707 North Halsted
312-440-1203

The Mother-Infant Connection is a 6-week discussion group for first-time moms with babies who are not yet crawling. Child development specialist Karen Benson leads the new mom groups in discussions on sleeping, feeding, and adjusting to motherhood. Karen creates an intimate and casual environment in which new moms can find their own voice as a mother. Most mother-infant groups continue to meet independently after the 6 weeks are completed. The fee is $60 and free parking is available in a lot across the street.

New Moms Support Group

Prentice Women's Hospital

Northwestern Memorial Hospital

333 East Superior Street

312-926-8400

www.nmh.org/maternity

Although the New Moms Support group is operated by Prentice Women's Hospital it is open to all new moms regardless of where they deliver. In addition to this group, Prentice runs "Transitions to Motherhood" (see below). Prentice Hospital will screen inquiring new moms to determine which group best suits each mom. The New Moms Support Group is run by a psychiatrist and helps moms who are having a more difficult transition with motherhood. This group has more of a group therapy feel to it and offers the necessary support that many women need. Babies are cared for in a separate room. The group runs for six weeks and is $120.

Northside Parents Network (NPN)

1218 West Addison Street

312-409-2233

www.northsideparents.org

As a former co-director of the Northside Parents Network (NPN), I cannot say enough good things about this organization. When my daughter was four months old and I was going a bit crazy in my isolation, I found this group and began attending their weekly drop-ins with my daughter. Some of the women I met there are still among my closest friends and integral members of my parenting community. NPN offers a number of great programs for parents with young children including new mom's groups, neighborhood social clubs, a dad's group, a single mom's group, a newsletter, a babysitting coop and educational programs. NPN is probably best known for the *School Information Booklet,* a guidebook on preschool and elementary schools on the northside of Chicago. Membership is a bargain at $30 a year—join today, you won't regret it!

ParentPrep

773-725-5610

www.parentprep.net

ParentPrep's motto is "until there's a degree in parenting, ParentPrep is here to help." It makes good on this promise by placing a number of valuable services under one "virtual" roof, including life coaching for moms, tutelage in taking better baby pictures and assistance in preserving and showcasing them, financial consultation, fitness, pregnancy massage and infant massage. Its services are offered individually, as well as through workshops and educational programs.

Rogers Park Mom's Group

773-764-4131 (ask for Ellen)

The Rogers Park Mom's Group has been going strong for ten years. Parents gather twice a month (except for the summer months) to hear a presentation on a child, marriage or other mom-oriented topics. There is also time for discussion and casual socializing. Meanwhile, the children play while a sitter cares for them (children are separated based on ages, birth to three or three to five). During the summer months the group meets weekly to play at the beach or elsewhere. It is free and babysitting is just $5 for the meeting time.

The Savvy Mom

Belinda Lichty Clark
847-525-6863

www.savvymomseminars.com

The Savvy Mom is the brainchild of Belinda Lichty Clark, a former senior editor for iParenting.com and *Pregnancy, Baby Years* and *Women's Health and Fitness* magazines. The Savvy Mom seminars are—information meets baby shower! At the seminars pregnant women or new moms receive expert information and practical tips on a variety of parenting topics in a fun and social setting. Expert speakers cover a range of topics from beauty and wellness to nutrition to babyproofing, The Savvy Mom offers useful information in a fun and informal setting that brings women together to share their thoughts on pregnancy, parenting, and for a bit of pampering! Seminars cost $40 per person; they include a meal and a super gift bag.

The Sleeping Child

312-458-0601

www.thesleepingchild.com

The Sleeping Child is a program designed by Hans Lonnroth to help babies and their families get a good night's sleep. Hans has a master's level degree in social work but, most importantly, is a parent whose idea for this program came out of the struggles he had trying to get his son to sleep. There are many different philosophies on babies/toddlers and sleeping and Hans can help families struggling with sleep issues to understand the pros and cons of various methods, clarify their own feelings on this controversial topic and customize a plan for their family. He also will provide a sleep consultation that includes a 90-minute evaluation, the development of a sleep plan and unlimited follow-up (over the phone) for $195. For expectant parents or new families, Hans educates them about sleep issues and offers tips to avoid sleep problems. This program includes one in-person visit and up to three follow-up calls for $95. Lastly, Hans conducts educational talks to parenting groups or at public venues.

Sweet Pea's Studio

3717 North Ravenswood
Suite 213
773-248-YOGA

www.sweetpeasstudio.com

In addition to the wealth of programming Sweet Pea's Studio offers expectant moms, it provides great programs for new parents. The studio has workshops on topics such as breastfeeding, infant massage, selfcare for new moms and sign language for the family. Ongoing programs include new mom's support group, attachment parenting, baby & me yoga, busy baby yoga and music classes.

Transitions to Motherhood

Prentice Women's Hospital
Northwestern Memorial Hospital
333 East Superior Street
312-926-8400

www.nmh.org/maternity

This group is open to any new mom regardless of where she delivers. During this program new moms get a chance to relate to one another and share their stories, joys and struggles. Guest speakers also are invited in to discuss common new parent concerns, such as sleeping, feeding and marital issues. Babies are welcomed to accompany their moms to class! The class runs for a 6-week session.

Virginia Frank Child Development Center
3033 West Touhy Avenue
773-761-4550

The Virginia Frank Child Development Center offers a number of very good programs to assist families. There are drop-in groups for parents and children five and under. The gatherings, run by social workers, are offered three times a week for a fee of $7. The center also offers a terrific family life education series, which features a variety of informational programs for first-time moms, single parents, parent support for children with special needs, and more. It also has a Therapeutic Nursery School for children with emotional or developmental special needs and provides assessment and evaluation of children. A sliding fee scale is available.

Parent & Baby's First Class

Chapter 7 contains an abundance of information about classes that you and your baby can take together. Some of these classes begin as early as infancy but most are geared toward slightly older babies (three months and up) and toddlers. Listed below is information about two programs that you and your newborn can attend as soon after birth as you desire. These are special classes created specifically for newborns and parents.

Chicago Waldorf School
1300 West Loyola Avenue   www.chicagowaldorf.org
773-465-2662
Ages newborn–one year

The Chicago Waldorf School, known for its "whole child" approach in which the child's mind, body and spirit are all addressed, now offers an infant-parent program. These classes, led by a Waldorf teacher, are offered in 10- to 14-week sessions, depending on the time of the year and costs between $300 and $375. In these classes, parents nurture their infants and participate in "circle time" during which parents recite rhymes, sing, do gentle movements and show their babies age-appropriate toys. In addition to these activities, the teacher discusses child development and parenting issues.

Starbaby
"A Star is Born"
"Twinkle Twinkle Little Star"
Christine Culbert, RN, BSN, CCE
1417 Hinman Avenue
Evanston
773-381-9728
Ages newborn–crawling

The "A Star is Born" class series is the perfect way to kickoff your love affair with your baby. Christine, who also offers prenatal classes, provides a sanctuary for parents and their newborns. It is difficult to convey the gentle, intimate environment she creates. For example, Christine brings homemade bread to snack on and speaks in a quiet soothing voice as she recites songs, stories and poems then delights in each baby's reactions, movements, and expressions. Every week she lights a birth candle and gives each parent the stage to share their "birth story' with the group. The class series continues when crawlers graduate to the "Twinkle Twinkle Little Star Class." Sessions are 8 to 10 weeks ($15 per class) and well worth the trip to Evanston.

Hotlines

(Listed Alphabetically)

There may come a time where you need help and you need it immediately. Fortunately, there are a number of wonderful organizations that operate hotlines to provide immediate assistance (in most cases). Many of the hotline numbers I have included are local, though some are national. I have indicated if the hotline is available 24 hours a day. When it is not, I have provided the days and time that calls are answered. The hotlines listed below cover a range of topics from breastfeeding support to postpartum depression to prevention of child abuse.

Child Abuse Hotline (DCFS)
800-25-ABUSE

This hotline is available 24 hours a day to report suspected child abuse or for parents who are feeling very stressed and need to talk to a social worker.

Crisis Hotline
630-759-4555

This is a 24 hours a day, seven days a week, crisis "talk-line," where someone needing immediate help with a problem can talk to a trained specialist who will listen and give direction.

Illinois Poison Center Hotline
800-222-1222

The Illinois Poison Center offers immediate advice in cases of poison ingestion. It is available 24 hours a day, seven days a week.

La Leche League International
800-525-3243   www.lalecheleague.org

Call the hotline to locate a La Leche League leader in your area. She will counsel you through any breastfeeding struggles.

Medela
800-TELLYOU   www.medela.com

Medela is the manufacturer of breast pumps. By calling the above number or visiting its Web site you can locate the nearest distributor and/or receive help from a breastfeeding specialist.

National Child Abuse Hotline
800-4-A-CHILD   www.childhelpusa.org

This hotline is staffed by professional crisis counselors and it's available 24 hours a day, seven days a week for parents who need support or assistance to stop or prevent child abuse.

Parent Advice Line
Children's Memorial Hospital
800-KIDSDOC (Parenting and child health information 24 hours a day)

Children's Memorial Hospital offers a great service for parents looking for quick, expert advice. The "Parent Advice Line" is available 24 hours a day. Your first step to using this service is to call the above number and request a booklet. The booklet covers every imaginable health and behavior issue for newborns through teenagers. For example, if you want information on bug bites, dial the main number, then enter the corresponding access code and you will hear a detailed message about this topic, plus follow-up advice. It's an incredible resource and absolutely free!

Postpartum Depression Crisis Line
Northwestern Prentice Women's Hospital & Maternity Center
312-926-8100

This service provides trained intake workers who can assess a woman experiencing postpartum depression, determine immediate needs and provide direction.

Postpartum Depression Illinois Alliance
847-205-4455   www.ppdil.org

This organization provides information and resources for women suffering from postpartum depression. Calls to the crisis hotline are returned within 24 to 48 hours. The Web site also lists resources.

Northwestern Prentice Women's Hospital & Maternity Center Breastfeeding & Postpartum Help Line
312-926-7155

This help line is an invaluable resource for all new moms, regardless of where you deliver. The line is open seven days a week (8:00 AM–3:00 PM Monday–Friday and 8:00 AM–noon on weekends) to answer questions regarding feeding and caring for your baby.

Seat Check
866-SEAT CHECK   www.seatcheck.org

Seat Check is a national program that tells parents where they can go to ensure their baby's car seat is properly installed. Calls are answered between the hours of 8:00 AM and 5:00 PM central time. Visit the Web site or call the above number to find a location nearest to you. Their Web site also provides safety tips and information about car seat recalls.

A few words on postpartum depression . . .

Postpartum depression affects many new moms. Often new moms suffer unknowingly from it and feel tremendous guilt for having negative feelings about their new baby or motherhood. Postpartum depression ranges from a fairly minor to an extremely serious condition known as postpartum psychosis. Symptoms of postpartum depression include but are not limited to feeling afraid, anxious, lonely, fatigued, numb, panicky, hopeless, loss of concentration, panic attacks, feeling that your baby would be better off without you, scary thoughts, preoccupation with death, and fears of harming yourself or your baby.

The good news is that there are many places to turn to for help. This book contains hotline numbers and Web sites where you can find information and help. Also, your obstetrician or midwife or child's pediatrician can provide support. The key is to tell someone how you are feeling so that you can get the help you need and deserve.

Help in the Kitchen!

Dinner Is Solved
Chef Roger Greene   www.chefrogergreene.com
4412 North Damen
773-334-0517

I love this idea! For a fee of $350, Chef Greene, a 20-year veteran, will prepare five recipes (each one has four servings) in the comfort of your home. No postpartum mom has the energy to cook; yet, healthy meals are a must to a speedy recovery and the successful establishment of a breastfeeding mom's milk supply. This is an expensive service but would make a great group gift!

Savory & Sweet Specialties
Chef Molly Evans   www.savorysweet.com
773-612-6367

Chef Molly Evans graduated from Kendall College's School of Culinary Arts in 2003 and launched her own personal chef service business. Molly will shop for and prepare healthy, delicious meals in your home—a great relief to any new family. A small package includes three meals for two adults for $150, plus the cost of food. Molly brings her own equipment, cooks the scrumptious meals, provides reheating instructions and cleans up, of course! Larger packages are available too.

Seattle Sutton's Healthy Eating
15 locations in Chicago   www.seattlesutton.com
800-442-DIET

Seattle Sutton's Healthy Eating has a reputation for being "diet food" but it's more than that. Seattle Sutton's offers healthy eating plans made with fresh foods. One drawback is that the menus are predetermined. However, in a 5-week period there are no repeats. You can order a minimum of a week's worth of food, which includes breakfast, lunch and dinner. For one person the plan costs $106 for a week; a second person can be added for a $10 discount for both people. Seattle Sutton's offers a 1200 and a 2000 daily calorie plan; if you're a breastfeeding mom you will need the 2000 calorie plan. Meals are picked up twice a week.

Urban Fridge
2679 North Lincoln Avenue   www.urbanfridge.com
773-580-7495

You just had a baby and you need food but not the stress of preparing meals. Contact Urban Fridge! Chef Pete Repak and his wife, Debbie, are the owners. Pete has 15 years of experience as a chef at some of the country's top restaurants, including Charlie Trotter's, Fox & Obel Food Market, The Four Seasons, and The Mansion on Turtle Creek. Best yet, Urban Fridge offers a children's menu with real kid-pleasers, such as cheese ravioli, chicken fingers, and macaroni and cheese, all without those icky green garnishes. Adult meals (including a main course and sides) range in price from $8.79 – $11.99. All children's meals are $3.99.

Support Groups

Adoption

Adoptive Families Today
847-382-0858 www.adoptivefamiliestoday.org

Adoptive Families Today is a support group based in the northwest suburbs for prospective and adoptive parents and adoption professionals. Membership is $40 a year and members receive a newsletter, and can participate in child-friendly activities such as playgroups and holiday parties. Currently, there is no Chicago playgroup, but there is one on the North Shore that Chicago families attend.

Chicago Area Families For Adoption
630-585-4680 www.caffa.org

This organization provides support and advocacy for Chicago area adoptive families. For a membership fee of $30 a year it offers educational workshops, support groups, playgroups and a newsletter.

The Cradle
2049 Ridge Avenue www.cradle.org
Evanston
847-475-5800

The Cradle is a wonderful organization for families looking to adopt. Even if you adopt from somewhere else it offers terrific programs for adoptive families. Educational programs include biracial adoption, international adoption and adoptive family workshops. It also offers family counseling to help with the transition of adopting a child. Visit the Web site to find out more about the programs offered.

Twins, Triplets and More!

The Parents of Multiples Club
Northwestern Prentice Women's Hospital & Maternity Center www.nmh.org/maternity
333 East Superior Street
877-926-4NMH (4664).

The Parents of Multiples Club is available to parents of multiples or those expecting a multiple birth. It was created so parents can meet other parents and exchange ideas and/or concerns. Parents also benefit from educational lectures on a variety of topics such as promoting individuality among multiples, infant nutrition, infant sleep habits and saving for your children's college tuition. The program is ongoing, free of charge and available only to families who deliver at Prentice Hospital.

Children With Special Needs & Their Families

Autism Society of Illinois
630-691-1270   www.autismillinois.org

The Autism Society of Illinois offers parental support, information, referrals and educational conferences. It provides parent support groups in both English and Spanish. Parent support groups are offered on the southside of Chicago and in Skokie.

Chicago Association for Retarded Citizens (CARC)
312-346-6230

This organization provides parent support and outreach services for children and individuals who have developmental disabilities.

Deaf Access Program
TTY: 773-257-6289
Warmline: 773-257-5125

The Deaf Access Program has a pediatric program for deaf or hard-of-hearing children. This program has physicians on staff whom are experts in deafness, offers centralized services for deaf patients, provides referrals for specialty care and has family and group therapy.

Down Syndrome Clinic of LaRabida Children's Hospital
773-753-8646   www.larabida.org

The Down Syndrome Clinic of La Rabida provides medical and developmental evaluations and resources for parents and pediatricians caring for children with Down Syndrome.

Family Resource Center on Disabilities
20 East Jackson Boulevard, Room 900   www.frcd.org
Chicago, IL 60604
312-939-3513

This group offers parent education and training for parents of children with any type of disability. The Family Resource Center informs parents of their rights, explains how to obtain help and provides referrals. Trainings and individual assistance are free.

National Down Syndrome Society
800-221-4602   www.ndss.org

The society provides information and resources for families who have a child with Down Syndrome. It also provides contacts for local support chapters.

Gay & Lesbian Parenting

Family Pride

www.familypride.org

Family Pride is a national organization that works to support and advance lesbian and gay parents through community building, advocacy and local parenting groups (see Rainbow Families of Illinois).

Rainbow Families of Illinois

773-472-6469, ext. 464

www.rainbowfamilies-il.org

Rainbow Families of Illinois is a non-profit, community-based organization that includes lesbian and gay parents, their children and those considering parenthood. This informal organization of about 150 families sponsors monthly family-friendly events and occasional informational forums on a variety of topics. Membership is $40 a year.

Birthways, Inc.

1473 West Farragut

www.birthwaysinc.com

773-506-0607

Birthways hosts a monthly meeting of the group, "Not Yet Parents," that features guest speakers to discuss legal and health issues, among others, on becoming parents. Birthways also is home to a children's playgroup run by the Gay, Lesbian, Transgender & Bisexual group. Contact Birthways for exact meeting dates and times for both groups.

Single Parenting

The National Organization of Single Mothers

www.singlemothers.org

This national organization publishes a bi-monthly newsletter and has a terrific Web site that offers on-line message boards, chat rooms, advice, advocacy and support.

Parents Without Partners

800-637-7974

www.parentswithoutpartners.org

This group provides support and friendship for single parents through local chapters, a newsletter and online resources. Visit their Web site to find a local chapter.

Single Mothers by Choice

312-409-2229

Members of Single Mothers by Choice receive a list of other mothers in their area, a quarterly newsletter and more for $55 a year.

Support for Parents Who Have Lost a Child

SIDS Alliance of Illinois
800-432-7437   www.sidsillinois.org

SIDS is a national organization with a chapter in suburban Illinois that supports families who have experienced the sudden and unexpected death of an infant (up to one year). The SIDS Alliance of Illinois has a formal support group that meets in Hinsdale. In addition, it offers "Peer Parents," parents and/or grandparents who are trained to help newer parents.

Together in the Loss of a Child (TLC)
Northwestern Prentice Women's Hospital & Maternity Center   www.nmh.org/maternity
333 East Superior Street
877-926-4NMH (4664)

Should the absolute worst happen to a parent, the death of an infant (either late in pregnancy or in that first year), Northwestern Hospital provides a parent support group. The format offers discussion and educational speakers.

Chapter 4

Get Ready to Shop

~ Maternity Fashions ~ Baby Furniture & Equipment
~ Children's Clothing ~ Toys & Books
~ Specialty Stores ~ Services

When you start thinking about all the *stuff* you'll need for your pregnancy and new baby the list can seem daunting. It is easy to get overwhelmed by the list of items that some books say you need and by the images of perfect nurseries and idyllic playrooms in magazines and on television. First of all, it doesn't all have to be done at once. You will not need many of the items highlighted in this chapter until your baby is past her infancy. Secondly, when you purchase big-ticket items such as a crib or a dresser make sure to select one that will look as charming in a toddler's bedroom as in a newborn's nursery. Lastly, borrow as many items as possible, this goes for maternity clothes, children's clothing, baby furniture and supplies.

In this chapter I've divided the different types of items you will need by categories beginning with you and your maternity clothes. Next up is baby furniture and equipment, children's clothing, toys, books, specialty items and services.

Maternity Fashions

Thankfully, maternity clothes are more stylish and accessible than ever before. When I was pregnant I was limited to the specialty maternity boutiques, which I found to be a bit expensive. These days everyone is designing maternity clothes. For example, the Gap and Old Navy now sell maternity clothes. How many maternity clothes you will need depends on the type of work you do. For instance, will you need a dressy, professional wardrobe in addition to casual weekend clothes or can you get away with purchasing just casual items? Also, you need to consider the time of year you will deliver; if you are lucky you will require only one season of clothes, winter or summer. However, if you deliver in July or August you will need both winter and summer clothes because spring arrives so late in Chicago.

Most maternity stores offer similar exchange policies: items can be returned for store credit or exchanged within seven to 10 days of purchase.

Boutiques

Belly Dance Maternity
1647 North Damen Avenue   www.bellydancematernity.com
773-862-1133

Belly Dance Maternity is the best thing to happen to style-conscience Chicago moms-to-be. These hip maternity clothes are sure to thrill. Belly Dance is an upscale store that features clothes from designers Michael Stars, L'attesa, Nom, Cadeau, Olian, Diane von Furstenberg, JWO, Earl Jeans and much more. Clothes range in price from mid $40's and up for tops, dresses from $75 and up and pants from $42 and up with designer jeans from $160 and up. The store also sells diaper bags, nursing bras, maternity panties and sexy maternity lingerie . . . everything an expectant mom needs to spend her pregnancy in style! Clothes also can be purchased online. The store is family friendly with toys for kids, comfy chairs for dads-to-be (or tired moms-to-be) and a bathroom. Street parking.

Hot Mama
1963 North Sheffield
773-244-2070

Hot Mama is a spacious new maternity store in Lincoln Park. The store has a fantastic selection of clothing by Japanese Weekend, Olian, Duet, Annette B and Notice. It offers adorable ribboned t-shirts by "A Wish," for which some of the proceeds go to the "Make A Wish Foundation." The store has everything a pregnant woman needs, including harder to find items like fancy dresses for black tie events, swim suits year-round, maternity undies, nursing bras and more. The store also sells adorable new baby gift items. Hot Mama offers a nice personal touch; customers receive thank you notes with a discount for future purchases. The store has a comfy couch for dads-to-be, and, of course, bathrooms. Tops and blouses cost from $40 to $70; dresses $80 and up; skirts $50 to $100 and jeans around $118. Street parking.

Krista K Boutique

3458 North Southport Avenue www.kristak.com
773-248-1967

Krista K sells highly stylish women's clothing and has a small maternity collection, which includes designs by Liz Lange, Diane Von Furstenberg, Rebecca Taylor, Samson Martin and Juicy. Krista K's is a high-end store; for example maternity jeans sell for $122 – $174. You will love the t-shirts and tank tops by Samson Martin that announce your due date—a question you are certain to get at least once a day throughout your pregnancy. Street parking.

Swell

1206 West Webster Avenue
773-935-SHOP

Swell is an adorable maternity boutique that shares space with ShopGirl, a women's clothing store. The boutique offers a large selection of stylish and expensive maternity clothes featuring designers such as Olian, Maximum Mama, Japanese Weekend, Pumpkin and a nice assortment of maternity jeans. Street parking.

Department Stores

Bloomingdales

900 North Michigan Avenue
312-440-4460

Bloomingdales sells the Belly Basics line of maternity clothing. It has an extensive selection, which includes Belly Basics "essentials" kits. These kits are designated as "sleep," "athletic," "weekend," "work" and "evening" clothes and have everything you need for one complete outfit. In addition to these kits Belly Basics offers many different styles of pants and t-shirts, packaged individually. Fee parking is available in the Bloomingdale's garage.

Carson Pirie Scott

1 South State Street, 3rd Floor
312-641-7000

Carson Pirie Scott has a large maternity department that features designs by Tomorrow's Mother, Noppies Maternity and Olian. Many of the clothes are casual, but the store also has dressy clothes and active wear. There is a large selection of bathing suits and sale items. No designated parking garage.

Marshall Fields

111 North State Street, 3rd Floor www.field.com
312-781-1000

Marshall Fields on State Street carries a large maternity line (the Michigan Avenue store does not). Most of the maternity clothes are by Mimi Maternity and include casual, work and dressy clothes. There is an extensive selection of maternity bras, panties and nursing bras too. In addition to the Mimi Maternity line, Fields sells maternity clothing by Sweet Pea and Steena. Reduced fee parking is available in the adjacent garage with validation.

Nordstrom
North Bridge Mall
520 North Michigan Avenue
312-379-4300

Nordstrom has a small selection of maternity clothes, all by Belly Basics. The Belly Basics items offered are similar to the ones sold at Bloomingdales but the selection is not as extensive. Fee parking is available in the Nordstrom's garage.

National Chain Stores

A Pea in the Pod
46 East Oak Street
312-944-3080
www.apeainthepod.com

Pregnancy just gets hotter and hotter! A Pea in the Pod is leading the charge with sexy dresses (around $200), great looking pants (starting at $100) and tops to show off your growing belly (starting at $75). Street parking.

The Gap
555 North Michigan Avenue
312-494-8580
www.gap.com

A maternity line is long overdue from the Gap! The Gap now sells maternity clothes both at its Michigan Avenue store and online. The clothes are casual, stylish and affordable. The Gap has its own approach to maternity clothing. It labels items as "barely showing," "truly showing," and "anytime" so that moms-to-be know what to wear and when. No designated parking garage.

Mimi Maternity
Water Tower Place
835 North Michigan Avenue, 7th Floor
312-335-1818
www.mimimaternity.com

Mimi Maternity has every type of clothing you need to enjoy your pregnancy from work clothing to casual items to bathing suits and lingerie. The store is affordable and offers special discounts if you buy multiple items from their "Essentials Kit." Pants start around $44 and shirts for $24. The store also offers a small selection of books, Medela breast pumps and breastfeeding supplies. Fee parking in the Water Tower Place garage.

Motherhood Maternity

5 North State Street
312-541-9210

1730 West Fullerton
773-529-0564

7601 South Cicero Avenue
773-884-1805

www.maternitymall.com

Motherhood Maternity offers moms-to-be stylish looks at very affordable prices. Pants start around $18, tops at $9 and dresses at $29. Once your baby is born the store also has a nice selection of breastfeeding clothing. Parking varies at each location.

Old Navy

35 North State
312-551-0522

www.oldnavy.com

Pregnancy has never looked so cute or been so affordable. The Old Navy Store on State Street has a large selection of maternity clothes and is the only store in the city to sell the maternity line. Not surprisingly Old Navy's maternity line includes lots of jeans, cargo pants, jean skirts and t-shirts—all of which Old Navy is famous for. The prices are great: jeans for $38 and two t-shirts for $24. It also sells exercise clothes, dresses, camisoles and more. No designated parking garage.

Target

2656 North Elston Avenue
773-252-1994

2939 West Addison Street
773-604-7680

4433 South Pulaski
773-579-2120

8560 South Cottage Grove
773-371-8555

www.target.com

Target has a terrific selection of maternity clothes, I only wish it had been available when I was pregnant! The Liz Lange line at Target offers great looking dresses for $20, stylish pants for $23 and blouses for $18. It also carries the "In(due) Time" maternity clothing line, which is more casual with nice looking tops and exercise clothes. Every Target has a large, free parking lot.

Furniture & Equipment

Your biggest expense in preparing for baby's arrival will be furniture and baby equipment. There are some items that are a must but many others are optional. It is easy to become overwhelmed when preparing for your baby's arrival, but keep in mind that you and your spouse or partner are the most important factors in your baby's life and no dream nursery can compete with the love you will give your baby.

So here are the must-purchase items: an infant car seat, a bouncy chair, a crib or bassinet, a front carrier or a stroller, a monitor (depending on how large your home is), a highchair, infant laundry detergent, and infant toiletries, which include diaper ointment/cream, nail clippers, baby wash, infant Tylenol and ibuprofen, and a baby thermometer. There are a number of other items that will make your life with baby easier but they are by no means essential. These items include a rocker or glider, a changing table, a baby swing and a pack n' play.

Baby Equipment and Safety

As you will see from the descriptions of the stores below, baby equipment is expensive. Any baby items currently on the market have met the Consumer Product Safety Commission's standards, however, if you are borrowing equipment check the Commission's Web site at www.recalls.gov to make sure that the item has not been recalled. Take this cautious step for any item that you borrow, for example baby swings, car seats, strollers, pack n' plays, you name it. Also, any time you purchase a piece of baby equipment you will find a card in the packaging that must be mailed to the manufacturer. By completing the information on the card and mailing it in you will ensure that the manufacturer has your contact information and can reach you should there be a recall. It is also a good idea to create one central file where you store all of the directions and warranties for the items you purchase. That way, if years later you need to set-up your crib for a new baby, or you loan your equipment to someone you will have the directions to ensure that items are put together properly.

Car Seats

The car seat is the most important purchase you will make as a new parent. There are an overwhelming number of selections—some extremely luxurious, including leather, sippy cup holders and funky animal prints. But before you choose a car seat by design preference go to www.nhtsa.dot.gov to ensure that the one you like received an "A" for safety. Also, keep in mind that infants younger than a year or less than 20 pounds need to be strapped into a rear-facing car seat. For babies and toddlers 20 to 40 pounds, the seat can be forward facing. Many car seats can do both these days so look for ones with this flexibility to get your money's worth. The National Transportation Safety Board recommends using booster seats for children weighing more than 40 pounds until they reach the age of eight or are four feet, eight inches tall.

Baby Furniture & Equipment Stores

Baby's Room/Child's Space
640 North LaSalle Street   www.babysroom.com
312-642-1520

6133 North Lincoln Avenue
773-583-8112

The Baby's Room solves every nursery need. It offers a variety of crib styles in various finishes. Crib prices start at $300 and go up to about $1000. Most cribs are available within a month; special orders take 12 to 16 weeks for delivery. Bedding can be purchased in set packages for approximately $150 and up, or can be specially ordered and take 6 to 8 weeks to arrive. The store carries dressers, changing tables, gliders and mattresses. The Baby's Room has a large selection of car seats including Peg-Perego, Graco and Britax. Their stroller selection includes Bertini, Dreamer Design, Maclaren, Combi, Peg-Perego and Graco. Other items available are baby swings, infant carriers, bouncy seats, high chairs, cradles, child safety supplies, bottles, Medela breast pumps and diaper bags. Finally, the store carries children's furniture including fun beds with slides and tents as well as other bedroom furniture. The LaSalle Street store has street parking only and the Lincoln Avenue store is located in a mall with free parking.

Ballin Pharmacy
3330 North Lincoln Avenue
773-348-0027

Ballin Pharmacy is a real lifesaver for new moms! Located in Lakeview, it is a family owned and operated pharmacy. The staff is highly skilled and very helpful. Ballin Pharmacy sells and rents Medela breast pumps. It also provides a wide assortment of breastfeeding supplies including Medela nursing bras, car adaptors for your pump, bottles, bra pads, milk storage equipment and much more. Ballin also stocks Jost Stockings and Carolon Stockings, which some women require during pregnancy to help with vein discomfort or complications. Ballin Pharmacy is a fantastic resource for breastfeeding moms!

Galt Toys + Galt Baby
900 North Michigan Avenue
312-440-9550

Galt Toys + Galt Baby has some of everything you need for your baby and child. The store sells a wide selection of strollers by Mountain Buggy, Maclaren, Aprica, Bertini and Zooper. It also carries Graco baby swings and car seats, bouncy seats by Chicco and the Svan Chair—a high chair that grows with your child. Galt Toys + Galt Baby also sells Avent bottles, Baby Bjorn carriers, stools, potties and accessories. Reduced fee parking is available in the Bloomingdale garage with validation.

Elizabeth Marie
3612 North Southport Avenue
773-525-4100

Elizabeth Marie is a very unique store that is difficult to categorize. Owner Elizabeth Marie carries a mix of infant clothing, baby accessories, custom bedding, furniture, blankets and more in her tiny store. The store specializes in personalized items including plates, pillows and wall art. Elizabeth Marie is also a designer who offers custom interiors for your baby's room or playroom (see decorating section for more information). Her store is open from 10:00 AM to 3:00 PM on Mondays, Thursdays, Fridays and Saturdays or by appointment. Street parking.

The Land of Nod
900 West North Avenue   www.landofnod.com
312-475-9903

The Land of Nod is equally enchanting for parents and children alike. Most parents experience a sense of nostalgia as they shop among items of their childhood, such as toy radios, marbles, classic stories and more. But believe me we never had it this good as children! The store has everything you need to create a playful nursery, child's room and/or a playroom. The Land of Nod is heavy on themes. The store carries bedding (beginning at around $200 for cribs), accessories and toys that create a complete look whether your child is into farm animals, horses, flowers or baseball. The Land of Nod has several different types of cribs starting at $599. In stock cribs are available within five to seven days, otherwise it takes about a month. The store also offers coordinating dressers, armoires, bookcases and changing tables. The Land of Nod has a terrific music and book selection that encourages lingering. The store is set up so that parents or children can listen to the music before they purchase or sit down and read a story before selecting a book. The store provides plenty of play toys for children while parents shop, and a large free parking lot.

Lazar's Juvenile Furniture
6557 North Lincoln
Lincolnwood
847-679-6146

Just past the Chicago city limits, Lazar's Juvenile Furniture has everything you need to prepare for your baby's arrival. The store carries strollers, car seats, cribs, beds, dressers, changing tables, baby swings, high chairs, bassinets, gliders and more. Lazar's has a great selection for each of these items; you have never seen so many strollers in one place! Stroller brands include Maclaren, Combi, Bertini, Inglesina, Peg Perego and Mountain Buggy. The car seat selection includes Britax, Graco and Peg Perego. Cribs start at $380 and go as high as $2000. Cribs take between 10 and 12 weeks for delivery. Lazar's also sells bedding sets, or bedding can be custom made, which takes about 10 weeks. Once your child grows out of his/her crib you will find yourself back at Lazar's to choose a big kid bed or bunk beds. Lazar's has a free parking lot.

Pottery Barn Kids
2111 North Clybourn Avenue   www.potterybarnkids.com
773-525-8349

We all know Pottery Barn Kids from the catalogue but visiting the store personally is fun, and helpful in making selections. Pottery Barn sells beautiful cribs (starting at about $399), a wide selection of bedding and every item you will need to create a charming nursery, kid's room and/or playroom. Dressers range in price from $499 to $699; rockers and gliders from $549 and up; changing table are $249 to $599. Their high quality furniture comes in a variety of woods and finishes. For an additional fee of $59 to $69 you can purchase a converter kit to turn your baby's crib into a toddler bed. Many cribs are in stock and available for pick-up the day of purchase. Otherwise, it can take anywhere from two to eight weeks for delivery. A delivery fee of $65 is charged and Pottery Barn will not set up the crib. In addition, the store carries beautiful wooden toys such as kitchen sets and tables. The store's child-friendly environment encourages children to play in the store while parents shop. Free parking is available in the attached lot.

The Right Start
2121 North Clybourn Avenue   www.rightstart.com
773-296-4420

The Right Start is conveniently located in the same shopping center as Pottery Barn Kids. It is a go-to destination for baby and toddler equipment because it offers one-stop shopping. The Right Start has a great selection of strollers, which include the following brands: Combi, Sprinter, Peg-Perego, Maclaren, Zooper, Sit-n-Stand and Swan. Strollers are $199 and up. The store also carries many lines of car seats and boosters seats and even has seats on display so your baby or toddler can try them out. Once your baby is crawling, The Right Start has all the baby-proofing items you need to make your home safe. Also available in the store are breastfeeding and other feeding supplies, baby monitors, bouncy chairs, baby carriers, high chairs, diaper bags, toilet training equipment, great toys and more.

Sears on State
2 North State Street
312-373-6000

Sears is a great place to go to get baby supplies and equipment. Sears sells strollers, travel cribs, swings, high chairs and car seats by Kolcraft, Graco, Eddie Bauer, Fisher-Price, Evenflo and Cosco.

You also can pick up smaller items such as baby bathtubs, monitors, breast pumps, toddler toilet seats and bassinets. Finally, there is a limited selection of coordinated cribs, changing tables and dressers. No designated parking garage.

Target
2656 North Elston Avenue   www.target.com
773-252-1994

2939 West Addison Street
773-604-7680

4433 South Pulaski
773-579-2120

8560 South Cottage Grove
773-371-8555

Once you become a parent you may find yourself making a monthly sojourn to Target to meet your baby's constant supply needs. Diapers, wipes, sippy cups, toys . . . it's never ending. Target is also a great place to get all your initial baby equipment. Target sells many different brands, including Graco, Eddie Bauer, Evenflo, Chicco and Safety 1st so you always have a nice selection of whatever you are shopping for. Target has strollers, high chairs, car seats, booster seats, pack n' plays, exersaucers, bouncy chairs, baby bathtubs and smaller items such as baby monitors, bottles, pacifiers, toiletries, baby towels, diaper bags and of course clothing and toys. You also can register at Target's gift registry, so would-be gift buyers will know exactly what you need. Each Target has large, free parking lots.

Children's Clothing

What is more fun than dressing up your beautiful baby? Chicago has wonderfully unique children's boutiques that will test your self-control. I've also included contact information and brief descriptions about department stores and other retail stores.

Boutiques

Active Endeavors Kids
838 West Armitage Avenue   www.activeendeavors.com
773-281-2002
Sizes 6 months–14

Active Endeavors features comfy clothes for active babies and kids. At Active Endeavors babies and kids can find great clothes to gear-up for Chicago winters or for hot summers on Lake Michigan. Outdoor clothing brands include Patagonia and Columbia. The store features snow boots, sporty shoes and sandals by Merrell and Columbia. Active Endeavors also carries high-end clothes by Petit Bateau, Zutano, Jean Bourget, Charlie Rocket and Quicksilver. Items can be returned for a refund within two weeks of purchase and up to a month for store credit. Street parking.

Camelot
2216 North Clybourn Avenue
773-472-7091
Sizes newborn–16

Camelot offers its customers the chance to outfit their children in the finest clothes, many of which are from France. This is a great place to buy a special occasion outfit, as many of the items are fancy and pricey. Featured designers include Absorba, Confetti, Valeria, Chabaria, Baratin, Petitfon, Biscotti, Clayeux, Cakewalk and Billtornade (a children's couture line where pants cost $120 to $200). This is a good place to bring grandma! The store offers a nice play area for kids. Items can be returned within two weeks for store credit. Street parking.

Jacadi Paris
Water Tower Place, 3rd Floor   www.jacadiusa.com
835 North Michigan Avenue
312-337-9600
Sizes newborn–12

This French store sells exquisite children's clothing, bedding and accessories. The outfits have that fabulously put together look which some of us are still striving for as adults. If you have ever imagined the day your child goes off to preschool or kindergarten these are the clothes you probably envisioned him/her wearing. The clothes are well made and children will get lots of wear out of them as the pants and skirts have adjustable waists to expand as your child grows. The store also offers some hard-to-find items such as sleep sacks, which now are recommended for babies to sleep in, and table seats, those miniature chairs that you attach to a table, very handy in restaurants. Items can be exchanged or returned for store credit within seven days of purchase. Fee parking in Water Tower Place garage.

Jordan Marie
North Bridge Mall, 3rd Level   www.jordanmarie.com
520 North Michigan Avenue
312-670-2229
Sizes newborn–4T

Jordan Marie has fancy outfits for babies and older boys and girls. It is a great place if you are shopping for a christening outfit (from $100 to $300) or any special occasion where you need to dress up your baby. Jordan Marie is also a terrific shop for finding a precious newborn outfit. The store carries exquisite layette sets, matching booties and receiving blankets. Special occasion items can be returned within three days for a refund or 14 days with a receipt for a refund or for store credit, without a receipt. Fee parking in North Bridge Mall garage.

LMNOP

2574 North Lincoln Avenue
773-975-4055
Sizes newborn–10

www.lmnopkids.com

LMNOP's recently expanded store means there's much more space for its charming and fun children's clothing. LMNOP sells unique onesies with statements such as "I'm not a boy." Featured designers include Bees and Dragons, Oinkbaby and K. Kauff-men. LMNOP is the exclusive distributor of Jane Baird diaper bags, which have baby/parent friendly features such as detachable changing pads and flexible bottle holders capable of accommodating bottles for baby or water bottles for mom. An outfit usually runs about $50 and coats are approximately $200. Items can be returned within two weeks for exchange or store credit; gifts can be exchanged for up to a month. Street parking.

Madison and Friends

940 North Rush Street
312-642-6403
Sizes preemies–juniors' 16

www.madisonandfriends.com

Madison and Friends sells high-end, unique children's clothing. The store offers sophisticated looks for girls from designers Juicy and Diesel. Boys look adorable in clothes by one of my favorite boy designers, Miniman. In addition to clothing, Madison and Friends carries accessories such as Baby Bjorn carriers, diaper bags and a good selection of strollers. There is a high-end selection of shoes, a few wooden toys, and a really nice layette collection. Street parking.

Mini Me

900 North Michigan
312-988-4011
Sizes newborn–10 for girls (only up to size 3 for boys)

Mini Me is a high-end store that carries girl's clothing up to size ten and boy's clothing up to size three. Brands include a large selection of Lilly Pulitzer, lots of Petit Bateau for babies and Brooks Brothers clothing for boys and girls. The store also has a few toys and board books. Items can be exchanged or returned for store credit for up to 30 days after purchase. Fee parking available in the Bloomingdale's garage.

Oilily Children

North Bridge Mall, 3rd Level
520 North Michigan Avenue
312-527-5747
Sizes newborn–12

www.oililyusa.com

Oilily makes outrageously adorable clothes in bright colors, busy designs and fun prints; however, you do pay a price for all this cleverness. Baby socks cost $12 a pair, a onesie can go as high as $48. Dresses begin at about $100. Boy's pants start around $68. A good place to show grandma! Items can be returned for a cash refund for two weeks or exchanged for up to 30 days. Fee parking available in the North Bridge Mall garage.

Psychobaby

1630 North Damen   www.psychobaby.net
773-772-2815
Sizes newborn–6x

This store is so much fun! Store owners Marlo Hoffman and Lisa Starbuck (two moms) successfully created a welcoming environment with toys for kids to play, a cozy spot for mom or dad to read to their child and a bathroom labeled "potty." The store features brands such as Acme, Lemon, Metropolitan Prairie, Dogwood and Paperdenim and Cloth. Psychobaby is not cheap; dresses are $40 and up and Paperdenim and Cloth jeans are $100, but it has good sales! For newborns and babies it carries adorable items such as Trumpette's seven-days-of-the-week socks in an egg carton and onesie sets from Bees & Dragons. Do not forget baby's feet; Psychobaby has Primigi shoes ($54), Geox ($56) and Puma sneakers ($54) for older kids.

The store also offers toys and unique books, including many wooden toys by Haba and puzzles by Melissa and Doug. Lastly, dads love this store (I know this from personal experience and word-of-mouth), maybe it is because there is nothing frilly about it. For example, Psychobaby offers a dad's diaper bag, "Diaper Dudes," in black or camouflage (it looks like a messenger bag). Psychobaby sponsors story time every Wednesday at 10:30 AM when all books are sold at 15 percent off. The store offers a full refund within two weeks; store credit is issued for items returned between two to four weeks. Street parking.

The Red Balloon Company

2060 North Damen Avenue   www.theredballoon.com
773-489-9800
Sizes newborn–8

The Red Balloon Company opened its doors in 1998 as a children's furniture store, selling decoupaged toy chests and handmade table and chair sets. It has since expanded to offer a large selection of adorable children's clothing. For example, a tunic and pant set for toddlers by Tea for $55. Boys also look adorable in clothes by Milk & Honey, such as the "Route 66" shirt for $38. The clothes are unique because they are fun without making kids look like they are trying to be trend-setting miniature adults.

The Red Balloon has a terrific selection of books, toys, room accessories and vintage pieces. The store has expanded its personalized service to include a small Web site and mail-order catalog. Items can be returned for store credit. Street parking.

Department Stores

Bloomingdales
900 North Michigan
312-440-4460
Sizes preemie and up

Bloomingdales offers an extensive line of children's clothing beginning with the layette collection. The store has a "Layette Consultant" who will help moms-to-be select a complete layette. The store does not sell baby or children's shoes. Fee parking is available in the Bloomingdale's garage.

Carson Pirie Scott
1 South State Street, 7th Floor
312-641-7000
Sizes preemie and up

Carson's has a huge children's department. In addition to clothing the store sells some toys from FAO Schwarz. Featured designers for babies and bigger kids include Oshkosh, Carters, Jane Seymour, Little Me and Tommy Hilfiger. No designated parking lot.

Lord & Taylor
Water Tower Place
845 North Michigan Avenue
312-787-7400
Sizes preemie and up

Lord & Taylor provides a large layette and children's clothing department. The store also sells a few toys. Fee parking is available in the Water Tower Place garage.

Marshall Fields
111 North State Street, 5th Floor
312-781-1000

Water Tower Place
835 North Michigan Avenue
312-335-7700
Sizes preemie and up

The Field's store on State Street has a more impressive children's department than the Water Tower location. The layette and baby collection is very fun with adorable clothing by Confetti, Baby Couture, Petit Bateau, Absorbe, Ickybaby, Kenzo and Zutano. The store features a sizable toy section called "Creative Kidstuff" that sells a wide assortment of toys, puzzles and arts-and-craft-activities. The shoe department includes a great selection of brands, such as Aster, Elefanten, Columbia, Stride Rite and Naturino. Fee parking is available at a reduced rate with validation in the adjacent garage.

Marshall Fields at Water Tower Place offers a large children's department and a nice selection of layette items. The store provides a wide variety of clothing from the traditional to more fun and funky styles. Field's shoe department is small. Fee parking is available in the Water Tower Place garage.

Neiman Marcus
737 North Michigan Avenue
312-642-5900
Sizes newborn–6x for girls, newborn–3T for boys

The layette and children's clothing collection at Neiman Marcus is high end. Not only can you find beautiful clothing, but you can literally buy your baby a silver spoon at Neiman Marcus. Neiman Marcus also sells beautiful, plush blankets and stylish diaper bags. There is a parking garage off of Chicago Avenue.

Nordstrom
North Bridge Mall
520 North Michigan Avenue
312-379-4300
Sizes preemie and up

The layette and children's department at Nordstrom's is fabulous. The store carries many clothing brands including their own. Nordstrom's is known for its fabulous shoe department. It includes great brands such as Stride Rite, Elefanten, Teva, Diesel and more. The store is very kid friendly with funny mirrors where your child can view his/her reflection, tables with coloring pages and crayons and a large screen television. Also, moms will appreciate the bathrooms, which provide a separate "Mother's Room," that features comfortable chairs for breastfeeding a baby and a changing table with a sink—nice! Fee parking in the adjacent garage is available at a reduced rate with validation.

Saks 5th Avenue
700 North Michigan Avenue
312-944-6500
Sizes newborn and up

Saks 5th Avenue has a fairly small but exquisite layette and children's clothing collection. As you would anticipate, the items are beautiful and very high quality. There is a great collection of dressy clothing for the tiniest babies to older children. Fee parking is available in the Saks 5th Avenue garage.

Sears on State
2 North State Street
312-373-6000
Sizes newborn and up

Sears on State carries Lands End, one of my favorite baby and children's clothing lines. Lands End offers some of the best outdoor winter clothes and accessories and the plushest cotton pull-on pants and onesies for babies. The store also sells clothing by Carters, Little Wonders and Healthtex. No designated parking garage.

Other stores

Most of the stores listed below have multiple locations throughout the city. Parking varies at each location.

Baby Gap/Gap Kids
555 North Michigan Avenue   www.gap.com
312-494-8580
Additional locations throughout Chicago
Sizes newborn and up

Is there anything I can say about Gap that you would not already know? I doubt it, so go forth and shop at Gap.

Carter's
1565 North Halsted Street   www.carters.com
312-482-8603
Sizes preemie–4T in clothing and up to 7 in sleepwear

Carter's recently opened a retail store in Chicago that features cute and very affordable baby and toddler clothing. The first 90 minutes of parking is free with validation in the adjacent parking garage.

The Children's Place
North Bridge Mall, 3rd Level   www.childrensplace.com
520 North Michigan Avenue
312-467-0715

39 South State Street
312-332-9111

Additional locations throughout Chicago
Sizes newborn–14

The Children's Place is a great and affordable place to get your children completely outfitted.

Gymboree

Water Tower Place
835 North Michigan Avenue
312-440-3166

www.gymboree.com

1845 North Clybourne
773-525-2080 (free parking, with validation in attached garage)
Sizes preemie–9 in girls, 7 in boys

Gymboree's clothing line is made out of super soft, plush cotton that your child will love. The store also sells shoes, accessories and a few toys.

Old Navy

35 North State
312-551-0522

www.oldnavy.com

1730 West Fullerton
773-871-0601

Additional locations throughout Chicago
Sizes newborn and up

Just like Gap, Old Navy has you covered from babyhood through adulthood. Old Navy has a great and constantly changing assortment of quality and affordable clothes.

Target

2656 North Elston Avenue
773-252-1994

www.target.com

2939 West Addison Street
773-604-7680

4433 South Pulaski
773-579-2120

8560 South Cottage Grove
773-371-8555
Sizes newborn and up

I am a big Target booster. Not only does it have a terrific selection of baby/children's equipment and maternity clothes but they also have a large and high quality baby and children's clothing department.

Resale Shop

The Second Child
954 West Armitage Street
773-883-0880
Sizes newborn–child size 14; maternity

www.2ndchild.com

This upscale children's resale boutique sells high quality clothing in great shape—for half to a third off the original price. Limited amounts of toys, furniture, equipment and maternity clothing are also available. If you are interested in selling items at the store you will receive a third of the sale price once the item is sold.

Shoes

Alamo Shoes
5321 North Clark
773-784-8936

Alamo Shoes is a favorite shoe store of parents on the northside of Chicago. A family shoe store, Alamo carries a wide selection of shoes for children, men and women. Brands include Elefanten, Stride Rite, Jumping Jacks, Merrell, New Balance, Keds, Columbia, Sorrels and more. Alamo offers great service and knowledgeable salespeople to ensure the best fit for your child. My favorite part of shopping at Alamo is that once my kids are set with their new shoes (and balloons) the salesman turns to me and asks, "Something for Mom today?" Free parking is available in the lot across the street.

Little Soles
2121 North Clybourn Avenue
773-525-7727

Little Soles is a cute shoe boutique that makes shoe shopping easier with a large train table to occupy the kiddies. Brands sold include Stride Rite, Elefanten, Nimi, Jumping Jacks, Munrokids, Bartek and Columbia. The store is located in a shopping center (next to Right Start and Pottery Barn Kids) that has free parking.

Piggy Toes
2205 North Halsted Street
773-281-5583

www.ptoes.com

Piggy Toes specializes in high-style, expensive European children's shoes. The selection is impressive and the store is very kid friendly. There are toys to play with and kids will like the colorful, funky styles. Brands include Naturino, Geox, AsterMod8, Buckle My Shoe, Moschino, Bumper, Oilily and Roberto Cavalli. Street parking only.

Toys & Books

Toy Stores

Building Blocks Toy Store
3306 North Lincoln Avenue
773-525-6200

This neighborhood toy store offers a wide selection of toys including, Lamaze, Lego, Groovy Girls, Thomas the Train, Melissa and Doug puzzles, Plan Toys, Haba, Chicco, Hello Kitty, Selecta and Kettler Tricycles. Building Blocks has the best Schleich animal collection I have encountered. The store has a small book selection, mostly board books. There are toys for children to play with while you shop. Street parking.

Cut Rate Toys
5409 West Devon Avenue
773-763-5740

Located in the far northwestern neighborhood of Edgebrook, Cut Rate Toys has been in business for 51 years. When you see the selection Cut Rate Toys offers at rock bottom prices you will understand why it has been so successful. Toy brands available include Playmobile, Little Tykes, Thomas the Train, Groovy Girls, Barbie, Lego, Fisher-Price, Melissa & Doug puzzles and much more. If you are in the market for a large, plastic item such as climbing equipment, a sand box, a playhouse or any type of riding equipment then Cut Rate Toys is the place to go! The store also supplies everything you need to get ready for a birthday party from cups and plates to party favors to wrapping paper. There is a parking lot behind the store and street parking. Combine a visit to the toy store with breakfast or lunch at the Edgebrook Coffee Shop & Diner (see restaurant section in chapter 6), which is just around the corner from Cut Rate Toys.

Dorby Magoo & Co.
2744 North Lincoln Avenue
773-935-2663

Dorby Magoo delightfully indulges your little prankster. Who doesn't love creepy ants, whoopee cushions, squirt cameras, disappearing ink, and the old snake-in-a-can-of-nuts trick? Dorby Magoo is also a great place to purchase party favors. The store offers an endless number of small bins with little treasures to stuff party favor bags. Dorby Magoo has limited summer hours, open only on Fridays from noon to 6:00 PM and Saturdays and Sundays from 11:00 AM to 7:00 PM but is open Wednesday–Sunday during the rest of the year. Dorby Magoo also hosts super fun birthday parties! Street parking.

Galt Toys + Galt Baby
900 North Michigan Avenue
312-440-9550

In addition to great baby equipment Galt Toys + Galt Baby carries a wonderful selection of toys by Lamaze, Sassy, Chicco, Bruder Trucks, Tumble Tree House, Schleich animals and barns, Hello Kitty, Thomas and lots of board books. The store will validate your parking in the 900 North Michigan Avenue parking garage.

Quake Collectibles
4628 North Lincoln Avenue
773-878-4288

My favorite toy store! Quake Collectibles answers the prayers of children infatuated with Star Wars, Spiderman, Superman, Batman and GI Joe. The store is a great spot to rediscover your old favorites too. Not only does owner David Gutterman have containers full of action figures but he also has classic never-opened boxed toys too. Prices are very reasonable and you will be extremely impressed with his vast collection. Hours are a bit irregular—opened mostly in the afternoons—so call for exact times. Street parking.

Thomas and Friends
Water Tower Place
835 North Michigan Avenue
312-335-9302

Thomas and Friends sells—you guessed it—Thomas the Train. Bring your Thomas-obsessed toddler to play in and shop at this store. Fee parking is available in the Water Tower Place garage.

Timeless Toys
4749 North Lincoln Avenue
773-334-4445

One of my favorite toy stores, Timeless Toys, is a large store with a great selection of toys. Brands include Plan Toys, Melissa and Doug, Brio, Lamaze and Chicco, just to name a few. Timeless Toys also sells harder-to-find items such as tree blocks and cooperative games. You will love the high-quality wooden castles, barns, dollhouses and pirate ships. It also offers a great arts-and-crafts section, lots of dress-up clothes and accessories, outdoor toys, scooters, tricycles, a nice book selection and a small number of tapes and CD's. Street parking.

Toys & Treasures, Inc.
5311 North Clark Street
773-769-5311

Toys & Treasures is a very cute toy store where you will discover all the kid-favorites, such as Thomas the Train, Groovy Girls, plush toys and more. It also features more unique items; for example, beautifully made layered wooden puzzles. The store sells a small and adorable selection of baby clothing, which includes the fun and funky Zutano brand. Street parking.

Toys Et Cetera
5211-A South Harper Avenue   www.toysetcetera.com
773-324-6039

2037 North Clybourn
773-348-1772

This is a large toy store with everything your baby through school-age child could desire. It has a great selection of Lamaze toys, Brio, Thomas the Train, Playmobile, Lego, Plan Toys and much, much more. Toys Et Cetera also carries a huge game selection. There are beautiful books and a large party favor section that parents will appreciate for both its affordability and breadth of choices. Parking is available in the parking lot.

Not a toy store but something even better....

Another Time Candy Store
953 West Webster Place
773-529-7900

This store is a kid's dream come true and a parent's nightmare—just kidding, but it is a place that will challenge children's and parent's negotiating skills. Another Time Candy Store sells old-fashioned candy (such as rock candy) and current favorites in bins. There are also stuffed animals for sale. The store is very charming and a bit of a throwback to olden times. Street parking.

Suckers Candy, Inc.
3265 North Damen Avenue   www.suckerscandyinc.com
773-549-1706

Suckers Candy, Inc. is a new candy store located in Roscoe Village. It is a spacious and adorable store where kids fetch a tin pail and fill it up with their favorite treats. The candy assortment is certain to evoke your childhood memories. Selections include candy rings, giant pixie sticks, rock candy, gummi worms, lollipops, bubble gum cigars, Fundips and more! In case your child is uncertain about a particular candy she is welcomed to try ONE before buying! Suckers Candy, Inc. is the perfect place to put together goody bags for birthday parties. The store supplies small Chinese containers for free that you can fill with tasty treats. There also are custom gift baskets that range in price from $20 to $40. Suckers Candy, Inc. has a great assortment of small, retro toys, such as wooden pop guns, bike horns, chattering teeth, kazoos and whoopee cushions. Adults are not left out of the fun. Suckers Candy, Inc. sells South Bend chocolates, sugar free candies and gourmet cookies by Flathaus to please more sophisticated palates.

Chain Toy Stores

The Disney Store
717 North Michigan Avenue
312-654-9208
K-B Toys

Riverpoint Mall
1730 West Fullerton Avenue
773-281-5160

4620 West Irving Park
773-283-4852

Lego Store
North Bridge Mall, 3rd Level
520 North Michigan Avenue
312-494-0760

Toys "R" Us
3330 North Western Avenue
773-525-1690

www.toysrus.com

2551 West Cermack Road
773-247-4411

Independent Book Stores

Barbara's Bookstore
1350 North Wells
312-642-5044

www.barbarasbookstore.com

Marshall Field's location
111 North State Street
312-781-3033

Navy Pier location
700 East Grand
312-222-0890

1218 South Halsted
312-413-2665

Any Chicagoan knows that Barbara's Bookstore is a great local bookstore with a nice selection of books, friendly staff and fantastic children's books. Some of the locations offer children's story times; call for locations, exact days and times. Parking varies at each location.

The Book Cellar
4736-38 North Lincoln Avenue
773-988-2419

The Book Cellar is a terrific new addition to the northside of Chicago. The staff are very child-friendly and encourage children and their parents to linger and read stories. When I was there with my son a staff member brought out cushions for us to snuggle on while we read. The Book Cellar currently offers story time on Fridays at 11:00 a.m. with the "Storybook Mom." Lastly, kids and parents alike will enjoy the small cafe that features snack foods and light lunch options. Street parking.

Children in Paradise
909 North Rush
312-951-5437

Children in Paradise is a great bookstore dedicated solely to children's literature. The store offers board books, many paper covered picture books (a good bargain), and beautiful picture books in hardcover. Books are uniquely displayed throughout the store. For example, the store's potty books are displayed on top of a potty (no longer in use, of course). Story hour sessions occur on Tuesday and Wednesday mornings. The store provides a nice play area for children looking for entertainment while mom and/or dad shops for great books. Finally, there is a great bathroom with an incredible wall mural depicting an undersea scene that captivates children, so plan on spending longer than usual in the bathroom. Customers can get their parking tickets validated if they park in the 900 North Michigan garage.

Women & Children First
5233 North Clark Street   www.womenandchildrenfirst.com
773-769-9299

Women & Children First is an institution in Andersonville. This wonderful bookstore carries large children and parenting selections in a nurturing environment. Every Wednesday at 10:30 AM, store owner Melinda hosts a fun and engaging story time for children. We go whenever we can! The store provides the largest selection of children's picture books with paper covers that I have discovered—making it more affordable to buy all of your children's favorites! Street parking.

57th Street Books
1305 East 57th Street
773-684-1300

57th Street Books is a neighborhood treasure. The bookstore has a terrific children's section and provides twice-weekly storytelling sessions. 57th Street Books also participates in the annual Children's Book Festival in late September (see calendar of city celebrations). Street parking.

Chain Bookstores

Barnes & Noble Booksellers
www.barnesandnoble.com

Listed below are several Barnes & Noble stores located in Chicago. All of them offer weekly story hours; call for exact days and times.

1441 North Webster
773-871-3610

659 West Diversey Parkway
773-871-9004

1130 North State
312-280-8155

Borders Books, Music & Cafe
www.bordersstores.com

Listed below are the locations of Borders stores. Some of them offer weekly story hours; call for exact days and times. The North Michigan Avenue sponsors a children's story hour in Spanish as well as in English.

830 North Michigan
312-573-0564

2817 North Clark
773-935-3909

755 West North Avenue
312-266-8060

150 North State
312-606-0750

4718 North Broadway Avenue
773-334-7338

6103 North Lincoln Avenue
773-267-4822

1539 East 53rd Street
773-752-8663

2210 West 95th Street
773-445-5471

Specialty Stores

Dance Supply Stores

Dance & Mime Shop
643 West Grand Avenue
312-666-4406

When you go looking for the perfect (likely pink) leotard for your little ballerina, you will find it at the Dance & Mime Shop. It sells dancewear, shoes and costumes for the big show. There is street parking only.

Northwest Dancewear
6323 North Central Avenue
773-774-0400

Northwest Dancewear sells dancewear and shoes for ballet, tap and jazz. The store has parking in the rear or street parking.

Party Supply Stores

Doolins Amusement Supply Company, Inc.
511 North Halsted
312-666-8070
This party store has strong seasonal themes for parties and special occasions. There is a nice selection of typical kid-party fare whether you are looking for a pirate, princess or truck theme. Doolins sells balloons and party games too. A customer parking lot is located behind the building.

I've Been to a Marvelous Party
2121 North Clybourn Avenue
773-404-9400

I've Been to a Marvelous Party is a high-end party store with beautiful invitations, party supplies, favors and decorations. In addition to its vast selection of ready-to-go party invitations the store offers custom orders. The store also sells adorable birth announcements. I ordered both of my babies' birth announcements from I've Been to a Marvelous Party and was delighted with them. This store is located in the same shopping center as Right Start, Pottery Barn Kids and Little Soles—talk about your one-stop-shopping.

Card and Party Giant
1880 West Fullerton Avenue
773-342-1500

6253 North McCormick Place
773-478-6200

Affordable party supplies, invitations and balloons in every theme imaginable. Free parking in the attached lots.

Party City
1755 West Fullerton
773-525-0399

3417 North Western Avenue
773-871-3500

8141 South Cicero Avenue
773-582-5900

Affordable party supplies, invitations and balloons in every theme imaginable. Free parking in the attached lots.

School/Teacher Supply Store

The Learning Tree
4419 North Ravenswood
773-769-3737

This is a great store for purchasing everything your child needs for school. However, do not wait until your child is school age to visit. There are terrific educational toys, books and art supplies that children will love at any age. Street parking.

Services

Childproofing

By the time your baby is six months you will need to get busy childproofing your home. Baby gates, wall mounts on dressers and other furniture, cabinet locks . . . the list is huge. Experts recommend that you get down on the floor and do a room-to-room check for signs of potential danger. You can do this on your own and purchase child safety supplies at Target or The Right Start or you can hire an expert. The first time we baby-proofed our home we did much of it ourselves but eventually hired a handyman to install our cabinet locks and bolt our bookshelves to the wall. Should you wish to hire someone I have included a list of professional childproofers for you to contact.

ABC Baby Proofing, LLC
312-243-7233

The baby proofing professionals at ABC Baby Proofing offer a free evaluation of your home. After the evaluation, you will receive a report of their recommendations including the prices and the cost of installation, where appropriate. Families can then select from the list which items they want for their home.

Baby Solutions
400 North Racine Street, Suite 217   www.babyproofyourhome.com
312-733-BABY

Josh Berliant provides a free evaluation of your home and a list of recommendations to make your home as safe as possible. Clients can choose to have Baby Solutions install the recommended safety devices or purchase the necessary equipment and install it themselves. Safety devices also are sold on its Web site. Baby Solutions has been in business since 2000.

The Child Safety Company, Inc.
Northbrook   www.childsafetycompany.com
800-708-1648
847-498-7233

In business since 1991 The Child Safety Company has your family's safety needs covered. Aaron Ozorvitz offers a comprehensive in-home safety evaluation in which he goes room-by-room to determine possible risks to your baby. Sometimes his recommendations are as simple as moving items, while other times there are safety devices that can be installed to create a safer environment. After the evaluation the client receives a written report within 24 hours containing all the recommendations. The Child Safety Company sells devices that either the client can install or it will install them for the client. Ozorvitz is also a former Red Cross CPR instructor and medical first alert responder so he also reviews CPR with his clients. Call for fee information.

Safety Matters
Highland Park
773-281-2229
www.safetymatters.com

For a fee of $100 Safety Matters will conduct a thorough, room-by-room, evaluation of your home. Families then receive a list of recommendations. Safety First will install the necessary equipment or sell it to clients for them to install. It also sells safety equipment on its Web site.

Diaper Service

Should you choose to use cloth diapers there is only one company that provides delivery and pick-up services.

Bottoms Up Diaper Service
201 North Greenbay Road
Waukegan
847-336-0040

The Bottoms Up Diaper Service offers weekly pick up of soiled diaper (no need to even rinse them out!) and drop off of clean ones, which leaves you with more time to snuggle your little one. The price depends on how many diapers your baby requires per week. To give you a general idea, 80 diapers a week runs $16.45.

Decorating Services

Art As You Like It
866-733-0000
www.artasyoulikeit.com

Artist Jennifer Oleff, who trained at the School of the Art Institute, can transform your child's nursery or playroom into the magical space you envision.

Elizabeth Marie Black
Elizabeth Marie
3612 North Southport Avenue
773-525-4100

In addition to her beautiful store, Elizabeth Marie, owner and designer Elizabeth Marie Black offers custom interiors for your baby's room. She can do as little as you want or a "top to bottom" job," including rugs, curtains, furniture, pictures, lighting and more. She is great about accommodating your budget and incorporating items you already have. Elizabeth Marie is also known for finding whatever you want for your baby's room to make it unique, she has great sources and works with antique dealers across the country. She charges an hourly design fee. Her store is open from 10:00 AM to 3:00 PM on Monday, Thursday, Friday and Saturdays or by appointment.

Lisa Ficarra
773-784-6697   www.ficarramurals.com

Lisa Ficarra has been creating murals and decorative paintings in children's rooms and nurseries for more than 15 years. Her work was highlighted in *Better Homes & Garden 2003, Simply Perfect Kid's Rooms.* Lisa provides free consultations during which she will share her portfolio; pricing depends on the project.

Financial Planning/College Saving

College Illinois
www.collegillinois.com

College Illinois allows families to lock in tuition at today's rates, thus enabling parents of future college students to avoid tuition increases. You can start for as little as $45 a month. Families can enroll November through March of each year.

Bright Start
www.brightstartsavings.com

Every state now offers 529 Plans that enable parents, grandparents or others to save for a child's higher education. 529 Plans allow your investments to grow tax-deferred and distributions to pay for the child's college cost come out federally tax-free. The person who sets up the account has control over the funds and the funds can be used only for higher education expenses. Illinois' plan is called Bright Start, visit their Web site for more information.

Haircuts

Snippets Mini Cuts
2154 North Clybourne Avenue
773-755-1000

Snippets turns a child's haircut into an appointment with fun, complete with toys to play with while your child waits and videos to watch while she or he is getting a haircut. Older children can play videogames while having their haircut. When your child's haircut is done she or he gets a lollipop as a reward! It also offers a first haircut-memorabilia package complete with a video cassette of your child getting his/her haircut and a keepsake box to store your child's hair locks. Snippets accepts appointments or walk-ins; a haircut costs $20, but you can save money by buying multiple haircuts at once.

Hair Cuttery
2110 North Halsted Street
773-244-1947

www.haircuttery.com

3711 North Southport Avenue
773-832-9602

1675 North Milwaukee
773-328-7098

5160 South Pulaski Road
773-585-7127

Hair Cuttery charges $9 for a child's haircut. Parents will appreciate that children get a great cut at a great value and the kids like the lollipops. There are too many locations to list them all here. I have included a few stores in different areas of the city but to get a complete listing or to find the closest store to you visit their Web site.

Supercuts
324 South Michigan Avenue
312-341-9797

www.supercuts.com

1628 North Wells
312-944-7778

1129 West Berwyn
773-878-3700

6009 North Lincoln Avenue
773-274-0563

A haircut at Supercuts is just that, a haircut, no balloons, lollipops or videos. For $10.95 Supercuts can give your child a great haircut. There are too many locations to list them all here. I have included a few stores in different areas of the city but to get a complete listing or to find the closest store to you visit its Web site.

Photography

Living in Chicago we are fortunate to have an abundance of very talented children's photographers. There are certainly more than I could list in the book. I have included information about a handful of photographers that either friends or I have used and recommend. Almost all of these photographers will shoot in studio or on location, such as your home, the beach or a park. You can familiarize yourself with their work by visiting the Web sites when available. I have not included fee information because what you spend depends on whether you shoot your child's portrait in the studio or on location, if you request both black & white and color film, how many pictures you purchase and the size. However, prepare to put down some big bucks for your child's portrait as all of these photographers are very talented, but expensive. It is a decision you will not regret!

Mark Brown Photography
1331 West Fullerton   www.markbrownportraits.com
773-325-1133

Black & white and color photography; will shoot in studio or on location.

Byster Portrait Design
Arlene Byster
1730 North Clark Street
312-953-9512

Black & white and color; will shoot in studio or on location.

Chenevert Photography
Julie Chenevert   www.chenevertphotograhy.com
773-275-3633

Black & white; exclusively on location.

Classic Kids
917 West Armitage Avenue
773-296-2607

Black & white; exclusively in studio.

Marc Harris Photography
1875 North Milwaukee   www.marcharris-photo.com
773-342-1960

Black & white or color; will shoot in studio or on location.

Photography by Sher
3056 North Ashland Avenue   www.photographybysher.com
773-525-SHER

Black & white or color; will shoot in studio or on location.

Jessica Tampas Photography, LTD.
312-942-1905   www.jessicatampas.com

Black & white or color; will shoot in studio or on location.

Want something a bit different . . .

Patty Dvorak
773-450-4583   pdvorak@graphidea.com

Patty Dvorak offers a unique service if you are looking for something different than a photograph of your child. Patty paints magnificent portraits from photos. The best part is that your child will never have to "sit" to have her/his portrait painted. Patty works with a handful of pictures that the client provides. She likes to crop the pictures, then develops a sketch on the computer that the client approves prior to Patty painting the portrait. The process takes about two months. Portraits range in size; the average is about two feet by two feet. The fee varies depending on the size so call for information.

Out of Town Shopping

There is no shortage of terrific children's stores located outside of the city limits. In this book I have chosen to include a handful of places worth the drive because of the significant savings you will experience. So load up your girlfriends in the minivan and head out of town for a fun day of shopping and savings!

Land of Nod Outlet
1110-B Larkin Drive
Wheeling
847-459-9900, ext. 720

The Land of Nod Outlet has great deals on furniture and bedding. The outlet does not have the quantity that the retail store has but the inventory changes frequently so it is definitely worth a trip. There is a lot of bedding, some of which is marked as being "dirty" but inspect everything because most of the items I checked were not dirty or damaged. The day I went I bought a flannel comforter cover (that I had spied in the retail store the week before) for 70 percent less and it was in perfect condition. The furniture selection is a bit less reliable, much of it is damaged, but to varying degrees. The outlet has a nice amount of wall art and decorations. The store does not hold items and there are no returns. The outlet is open Monday – Saturday from 9:00 AM to 5:00 PM, except on Wednesday, when it closes at 1:00 PM.

Lighthouse Place Premium Outlets
601 Wabash Street
Michigan City, Indiana
219-874-4811

www.premiumoutlets.com

There is such a terrific selection of stores at this outlet shopping center and I always am delighted by the amount of money I save by shopping at Lighthouse Place. It is less than an hour and half drive from Chicago and well worth it! Below is a listing of the fantastic stores you will find at Lighthouse Place.

Carter's
219-874-4811

The Children's Place Outlet
219-872-0468

Ecco
219-879-4751

Gap Outlet
219-872-7673

Hanna Andersson
219-872-3183

K*B Toy Outlet
219-872-8882

Limited Too
219-879-9689

Little Me
219-879-9295

Nautica Kids
coming soon

Oilily
219-872-3577

Old Navy Outlet
219-878-0189

OshKosh
219-878-0942

Stride Rite Keds Sperry
219-874-2421

Tommy Kid
219-878-9888

IKEA

1800 East McConnor Parkway   www.ikea-usa.com
Schaumberg
847-969-9700

IKEA is a great place to meet many of your baby's and child's furniture and toy needs. About an hour north of the city, it too is worth the drive. Not only does IKEA have a great selection of cribs, toddler and big kid beds but it is also a fantastic place to shop if you are putting together a playroom.

IKEA is more than a shopping destination—it has the family-friendly thing down. Potty-trained kids can play in "Smaland" for 45 minutes while you shop. This place is a blast for kids with climbing toys, kitchen sets and more. The store provides a large cafeteria with kid's meals for $1.99 and individual jars of organic baby food are for sale! As if that were not enough it also has a great play area next to the tables so parents can eat in peace. Now, in the interest of full disclosure, I have to include my husband's perspective. He does not share my enthusiasm for IKEA because he says everything takes half a day to put together and with minimal instructions. A frustrating process but I still say it's worth it!

Chapter 5

From Childcare to Preschool: Finding the Best Caregivers for Your Child

~ Nannies ~ Au Pairs ~ Childcare Centers ~ Family Childcare Providers
~ Tots & Parents: Early Preschool Programs ~ Preschool

When I was pregnant, someone once asked me what was the best part of being pregnant and I answered, "that she is always with me wherever I go." I could not imagine a time when I could trust my daughter to someone else. But of course that time does come for all of us and you will need to be prepared.

Whether or not you plan to work full-time once your baby is born, there will be times when you just cannot take your baby with you. If you plan to work full-time, part-time or desire a regular time each week when you can go places without your baby then you will need to find childcare. Aside from the daunting task of finding good childcare, there is also the cost to consider. One option to pursue when trying to keep childcare costs down is to investigate if your employer offers a flexible spending plan that allows you to set aside pretax childcare funds.

In a city as large as Chicago, there are many childcare options depending on your family's needs, preferences and budget. But whether you are looking for in-home care or plan to take your child to a daycare center, you will need to do your homework in order to find the right person or place.

In my experience the best way to find good childcare is word-of-mouth. When I was co-director of the Northside Parents Network, I fielded many questions about how to find childcare. Among the advice I always passed on is to ask other parents, whether they be friends or just happen to be playing with their child next to you in the park.

Deciding what type of childcare is best for your family

Selecting a childcare provider is the most important decision you will make regarding your new baby. The first question you need to answer is what type of childcare will best suit your family's priorities, schedule and budget. You basically have four options: a nanny (live-in or come-and-go), an au pair, a daycare center or family daycare. No one can make this decision for you as it is a very personal choice, but to help start the ball rolling, I have described the options and included a list of places or people to contact once you decide what type of care is best for your family.

Nannies

The first question to consider once you decide you want childcare in your home is whether you should hire a nanny or an au pair. A nanny is a professional childcare provider who can either live in or come and go. An au pair is a student who's participating in an exchange program and your family will be her "host family."

Au pairs are not necessarily good options for families in which both parents (or a single parent) are working full time. Au pairs can work up to 45 hours per week, a restriction most parents working full time would find hard to accommodate. Also, au pairs can only work in the country for a year, which means your child and family will have to go through another difficult transition period when you need to hire a new childcare provider.

I have never hired a nanny but most of my friends who have, found their nannies through word-of-mouth. In fact, nannies themselves are often the best resource. I have one friend who has found each of her nannies through the neighborhood park just by asking other nannies whose approach to their charges she admired.

Community bulletin boards are another great source for finding childcare. Good locations to check out include any buildings where children's classes are taught, family-friendly restaurants, grocery stores, park districts, preschools and local coffee shops.

There also are many good agencies that place nannies with families. Nanny agencies often come and go at an alarming rate. You will note that I have included in each agency's description the length of time it has been in business. This is an important indicator of the agency's quality. Also, I have included only agencies that friends of mine have had positive experiences with.

If you decide to work with an agency you will pay a placement fee, though you determine the nanny's salary. Also, keep in mind that although the agency will have conducted an interview and background check you still must ask for, and check references for, any potential candidate.

Agencies

Below are nanny agencies, their contact information and finder fees.

American Registry
980 North Michigan Avenue, Suite 1400-46   www.american-registry.com
312-475-1515

In business since 1950.
Placement fee: $1400.

Childminders, Inc.
847-673-8998   www.childmindersinc.com

In business since 1988.
Placement fee: $1700/full-time; $900/part-time.

Lakeview Domestic Agency, Inc.
3166 North Lincoln Avenue, Suite 214
773-404-8452

In business since 1992.
Placement fee: one week's salary; 18-month guarantee.

Nanny Resource
4406 North Milwaukee Avenue   www.nannyresource.com
773-736-3173

In business since 1997.
Placement fee: Two week's salary/full-time; one and a half week's salary/part-time or live in; six-month guarantee.

North Shore Nannies
847-864-2424   www.northshorenannies.com

In business since 1991.
Placement fee: 10 percent of first year's salary; 90-day replacement guarantee.

Nurture Network
773-561-4610

In business since 1991.
Placement fee: Two week's salary or $800 (whichever is largest) full time; $600/three days per week; $400/ two days-per-week; 60-day guarantee; also provides three-day trials with as many nannies as desired.

There are a growing number of online nanny agencies. Again, I cannot recommend any of them but have provided the contact information to aid your search. They are as follows:

4nannies.com
800-810-2611   www.4nannies.com

This Web site is designed to assist parents in their quest for a nanny. Not only does it provide a list of nanny agencies, but it also walks parents through sample questions they should ask during the interview, explains what taxes parents must pay and makes recommendations about various background checks a family can make and lists companies that can conduct this research. This Web site is especially helpful if you hire a nanny on your own and want to conduct a thorough background check.

Sittercity.com
Over 500 babysitters in the Chicago area   www.sittercity.com
888-211-9749

Sittercity is a database of college babysitters. A membership fee is required to peruse its database, which uses a number of different search criteria, including times available, languages spoken, distance sitter is willing to travel, transportation preferences and more. You also can post jobs and maintain an online sitter list for quick reference. This site includes full-time, part-time and occasional positions.

TeacherCare
888-TEACH-07   www.teachercare.com

TeacherCare is an early childhood agency that places private teachers with families seeking full-time or part-time childcare in their home. TeacherCare childcare providers are educated in child-related fields such as infant programs, Montessori education, child psychology, special needs and gifted education.

Nanny Taxes

The Nanny Tax Company
Arthur Ellis
2149 West Roscoe
773-327-9100

Attorney Arthur Ellis began The Nanny Tax Company in 1995. Arthur takes the hassle and confusion out of filing your nanny's taxes. For example, to file nanny taxes you first must register with three different agencies and file 12 different forms—and that just gets you started, other forms must be completed quarterly and annually. Legally, anyone paying a domestic worker more than $1400 in a calendar year must pay certain taxes. Many families do not do this and you also may wonder why bother. Well for many reasons, the most important being that it is the law. There are several other important reasons to file taxes; for example, if your nanny wants to purchase a car or house she must be able to show evidence of employment; if she stops working for you she can file for unemployment; also she will be eligible for social security when she retires—all good things!

Au Pairs

An au pair comes to the United States to provide live-in childcare. When you hire an au pair your family is her "host family." An au pair lives in your home, which many families find to be a more affordable childcare option. Often families choose an au pair because they want their child to be exposed to a specific language. The downside of selecting an au pair is that they are young, usually inexperienced and only in the country for one year. Below are the names of four agencies to contact for more information.

Au Pair in America
800-928-7247   www.aupairinamerica.com

Au Pair USA InterExchange
800-AUPAIRS (287-2477)   www.interexchange.org

EF Au Pair
800-333-6056   www.efaupair.com

EurAuPair
Live-in childcare   www.euraupair.com
800-960-9100

Childcare Centers

When deciding what type of childcare is best, many families select a childcare center because it provides children with socializing opportunities, lots of stimulation and is more affordable than a nanny. On the downside, you and your spouse (or partner) will have to incorporate getting your child fed, dressed and out the door as part of your morning routine so you can get to work on time—a true feat! If you decide to go the childcare center route, you will need to diligently research many facilities, as there are major variances in quality.

The Illinois Department of Children and Family Services issues licenses to every childcare center and family childcare provider caring for more than three children. When you begin your search, plan on visiting many different childcare centers and take your questions with you. To get you started, I have included some questions below.

- How close is the center to your home and/or work?
- Does the National Association for the Education of Young Children (NAEYC) accredit the center?
- What is the adult-child ratio?
- How is discipline handled?
- Is there a minimum education standard for teachers?
- Does the center offer back-up care for sick babies?
- What is the center's late pickup policy/fee?
- What is the center's nap schedule?
- Do all staff members know infant/child CPR?
- Will you receive a credit for times when your family is on vacation? If it is a family daycare center you are interviewing, how does she/he set her/his vacation schedule?
- Is there an outdoor play area?
- Is there a different summer schedule?

More insight on finding the best childcare for your baby

Selecting a childcare provider is an incredibly difficult decision. Dr. Stanley Greenspan, a practicing child psychiatrist and recipient of numerous national awards, is world-renowned for his unique research and clinical work in child development. Dr. Greenspan is a founder and former president of Zero to Three: National Center for Infants, Toddlers, and Families.

Dr. Stanley Greenspan recommends that parents look for the following criteria when selecting childcare:

- Does this person provide safety and security?

- Is this a person who's warm and nurturing?

- Is this a person who has the time and energy (i.e., not overextended and caring for too many children)?

- Is this a person who's supportive and very interactive (i.e., reads babies' and children's communications)?

- Is this a person who can set limits but in a very gentle manner? If it's a verbal child, is this a person who is able to talk and interact in words and engage in play with children involving lots of verbal exchanges?

- Is this a person who seems to understand what children of different ages require so that they can tailor the care to the needs of the child?

Below are the names of some organizations that can help locate a quality childcare facility.

National Association for the Education of Young Children
800-424-2469   www.naeyc.org

When looking for a childcare center try to find one that has been accredited by The National Association for the Education of Young Children (NAEYC). The NAEYC is the nation's largest professional organization of early childhood educators. NAEYC accreditation for early childhood education programs is a strenuous process. Programs that receive NAEYC accreditation must meet the highest standards in early childhood care by creating quality programs that promote the physical, social, emotional and cognitive development of young children while responding to the needs of families. To locate an accredited childcare center in your area, visit NAEYC's Web site or call to request a catalogue.

Illinois Department of Children & Family Services

Chicago Headquarters   www.state.il.us/dcfs
100 West Randolph Street
6th Floor, Room 200
312-814-4150

The Department of Children and Family Services (DCFS) is responsible for licensing day care centers and home day care, which means that a DCFS licensing representative has inspected the facility and found it to meet the minimum licensing requirements. A license is valid for three years (though each facility is inspected annually) and must be posted. The license will indicate the maximum number of children allowed in the facility. By calling DCFS or visiting its Web site you can obtain a copy of the "Summary of Licensing Standards for Day Care Centers." This is a short, six-page document that identifies what to look for when selecting a center, such as the staff/child ratio and the maximum group size for each child's age group. Also, DCFS operates an information line (877-746-0829) that provides information on the past history and record, including substantiated violations of licensed day care homes and centers. The information line is operated Monday–Friday from 8:30 AM to 5:00 PM.

Action for Children

773-687-4000   www.daycareaction.org
Walk-in Locations:
Avondale/Logan Square: 2745 North Elston Street

Uptown: 4554 North Broadway Suite 320

Chatham/Grand Crossing: 8741 South Greenwood

The Day Care Action Council of Illinois produces a "Child Care Directory" for parents in both English and Spanish. The directory contains a list of childcare providers and resources by location. In addition, the guide shares vital information on laws governing children and childcare.

Cook County Child Care Resource and Referral (CCR&R)

773-769-8000   childcare@daycareaction.org

A good place to start when you embark on your childcare search is to contact the Cook County Child Care Resource and Referral, a joint program of the Day Care Action Council of Illinois and the Child Care Initiatives of Jane Addams Hull House. The referrals include childcare centers, in-home childcare providers and nanny service referrals. Parents in need of childcare can call the referral line, at which time a consultant will complete a family intake (a process that takes less than 10 minutes over the phone), provide information about selecting childcare and identify childcare providers who meet the family's criteria. Referrals are not given over the phone but are mailed. Families usually receive the listing in three to five business days. They can also fax it to you if you ask. Parents pay a one-time fee (free–$30 depending on income) for the year and may call for additional listings throughout the year. The referral line is open Monday–Thursday 8:30 AM–4:30 PM and Friday 8:30 AM–12:30 PM.

Child Care Chicago   www.thecityofchicago.com

The city's Web site has a section that provides the names, addresses and phone numbers of childcare centers, family childcare providers and preschools.

Early Childhood Network of Edgewater & Rogers Park
5533 North Broadway   www.earlychildhoodnetwork.org
773-769-1717

If you live in the Edgewater or Rogers Park neighborhoods and are looking for childcare, contact the Early Childhood Network of Edgewater & Rogers Park. The network produces a booklet called the CAMERA Guide, which provides listings of childcare centers, preschools, Head Start centers and childcare homes as well as other support services.

Family Childcare Providers

Some parents select a family childcare provider because they want the socializing opportunities that childcare centers can provide, desire a more affordable option than a nanny and/or want the smaller, more intimate environment that a family childcare provider can create. The Department of Children and Family Services must license family childcare providers who care for more than three children. Many families choose in-home childcare providers because they like the fact that their child will be exposed to other children of various ages as opposed to childcare facilities where children are often segmented by age groups. *For resources on how to find family childcare providers, refer back to the resource list for childcare centers as it also contains referral information for family childcare providers.*

Tots & Parents: Early Preschool Programs

Sometime between babyhood and your child's preschool days he or she will be the right age for a tot and parent program. These programs are often provided by preschools but do not necessarily help you get into that preschool. Word to the wise: these programs can be as difficult to get into as preschool. I have listed below just a few of the high quality and very popular programs offered in Chicago. These programs vary greatly in their approaches to early childhood education so take the time to research which one will best suit your child. Some of these programs begin as early as six months.

Chicago Waldorf School
"Parent/Child Program"
1300 West Loyola
773-465-2662
Ages 1–3

www.chicagowaldorf.org

Children of the Heart
Housed at Sacred Heart
6250 North Sheridan Road
773-743-8098
Ages birth–three

Children of the Heart is a bit different than the other programs listed in this section. It provides educational presentations for parents and playtime for children with their parents. The group meets twice a week and targets parents who might need extra support. The program also strives to create an economically and ethnically diverse program so any family residing near the school is welcomed to apply.

The Fourth Presbyterian Church Day School
"Twos & Parents"
126 East Chestnut
312-787-2729 ext. 282
Ages 2–3

www.fourthchurch.org

Near North Montessori
1434 West Division Street
773-384-1434
Ages 6 months–24 months

www.nnms.org

Park West Cooperative Nursery School
Parent Toddler Program
2335 North Orchard
773-327-1115
Ages 18 months–30 months

www.parkwestcoop.org

Sing n' Dance, Parent & Toddler Nursery School
Drucker Center
1535 North Dayton Street
773-528-7464
Ages 17 months–3 years

www.singndance.com

Preschools

Just when you thought you had it all figured out on the childcare front it is time to begin researching preschools. Thankfully, most preschools in Chicago do not require that you sign up the day your child is born but rather when your child is two in anticipation of him or her attending at three years of age. As with childcare centers and family childcare providers, there are too many preschools to list here. However, in your quest to select the right preschool for your child I have included some great resources for you to pursue.

Northside Parents Network (NPN)
1218 West Addison   www.northsideparents.org
312-409-2233

Among the many terrific services that NPN provides is its information on preschools (and elementary schools for that matter). Every other year, NPN publishes the School Information Booklet; last year's edition included almost 100 preschools and elementary schools. The book does not rate preschools but includes contact information, teacher/child ratios, areas of emphasis and cost. Call NPN or visit the Web site to order your booklet; it's $15 for non-members and $5 for members. In addition, NPN hosts several annual events each fall, including a preschool fair and a program on how to select a quality school program.

Independent Schools   www.independentschools.net

The Independent Schools hosts an annual school fair each fall. It is free and open to the public and a great way to learn more about private schools in Chicago. In addition, its Web site has contact information for some private schools in Chicago.

Chicago Public Schools
Tuition-Based Preschool   www.ecechicago.org/pages/home/programs/
125 South Clark Street   preschool/Tuition_Based_Preschool
773-553-2010

In the last few years 14 Chicago Public Schools (CPS) launched tuition-based preschool programs in elementary schools. The program is offered September–June for three and four year olds and features terrific facilities, with teacher/child ratios and equipment that rival private preschools. Tuition-based preschools are different than the state preschools offered by CPS. There are no specific qualifications needed to enroll and the program is fee-based. The program is full day (from 7:00 AM to 6:00 PM). Parents can choose to use it as a half-day program, though the tuition remains the same. To find out where these preschools are offered, visit the above Web site or call for a booklet. For the 2003–2004 school year the tuition was $175 per week.

Chicago Park District   www.chicagoparkdistrict.com
312-742-PLAY

Many Chicago park districts offer preschool programs. To find out which ones do, visit its Web site.

YMCA

Irving Park YMCA   www.ymcachgo.org
4251 West Irving Park Road
773-777-7500

Lakeview YMCA   www.lakeviewymca.org
3333 North Marshfield Avenue
773-248-3333

South Side YMCA
6330 South Stony Island
773-947-0700

Several YMCAs offer "Kiddy Kollege," for children ages two-and-a-half through five. Families can sign up for up to three days a week. The program offers socialization, crafts and movement. The program is $100 for members and $150 for nonmembers. Lake View YMCA, Irving Park YMCA and Southside YMCA offer this program.

Chapter 6

All Around Town: Adventures for Babyhood & Beyond

~ Museums ~ Big City Locations ~ Libraries ~ Theater & Musical Events
~ Drop-In Hot Spots ~ Dining Out

Having a baby brings out the child in mom and dad, too. All of a sudden you find yourselves exploring places and learning about things that have nothing to do with your work or "to do" list. Thanks to our children we get to be curious again. My daughter and I were visiting the Shedd Aquarium once when she was three. She asked me how dolphins sleep, which of course I could not answer. Moments later we spotted a marine biologist answering questions and my daughter asked her how dolphins sleep. Well it turns out they never completely sleep; one side of their brain shuts down and they continue to float along with one eye open and the other shut. Who knew?

We are fortunate to live in a culturally rich city, and having a baby is your ticket to explore everything Chicago has to offer. After all, it is your parental duty to enrich your child's life by exposing him or her to museums, theater (yes, kiddy theater counts), music and literature! So get out there with your child and enjoy.

Museums

Museum Memberships

I think it is well worth it to purchase museum memberships for the ones that you frequent. Many

museums have reciprocal memberships so it is best to do a bit of homework before purchasing any one membership. One of the best deals I have found is to purchase the annual "Explorers" membership from the Chicago Children's Museum for $110. When you join at this level you receive memberships to the Association of Science-Technology Centers and the Association of Children's Museums, which gets you into fabulous museums in Chicago and across the country, including the Field Museum, the Museum of Science and Industry, the Peggy Notebaert Museum, the DuPage Children's Museum, Wonder Works, the Adler Planetarium, Health World and Kohl Children's Museum. To learn more about which museums are members of these organizations, visit the Association of Science-Technology Center's Web site at www.astc.org and the Association of Children's Museum's Web site at www.childrensmuseums.org.

Great Kids Museum Passports

By far the most economical way to enjoy our museums is to visit your local library and check out the "Great Kids Museum Passports." These fabulous passes are good for one week and allow access to 11 museums including the Adler Planetarium, the Art Institute, the Chicago Children's Museum, the Chicago Historical Society, the DuSable Museum of African American History, the Field Museum, the Mexican Fine Arts Museum, the Museum of Contemporary Art, the Museum of Science and Industry, the Peggy Notebaert Museum and the Shedd Aquarium. It is important to refer to the museum information section in the brochure for each museum's admission guidelines. For the most part, admittance to the museums for family members is covered, but some special shows or exhibits may not be.

Adler Planetarium & Astronomy Museum
1300 South Lake Shore Drive   www.adlerplanetarium.org
312-922-STAR

For years I never visited Adler Planetarium, assuming it more appropriate for older children. I was so wrong! Upon hearing my daughter's rave reviews after a field trip, I gave it a try. Sure enough, my three-year-old loves it! Of course, there are many activities that young children cannot comprehend but there is plenty for them to enjoy. There are numerous brief 3-D movies about stars and planets for younger children. The longer (30 minutes) sky shows in the theaters are geared toward children six and older (but my three-year-old enjoyed it). There are lots of hands-on exhibits that stimulate young kids' minds such as how old they would be on Jupiter. There is a fabulous café with striking architecture and views of the city and lake. The offerings are served up cafeteria style. They include hot dogs, grilled cheese and PB & J. There are sandwiches, soups and salads for moms and dads. Admission is steep at $13 for adults and $11 for children ages 4–17. This fee includes your choice of one sky show. Admission to the Adler is free on Mondays and Tuesdays, September 15th–December 23rd but there is an extra charge for shows. Parking is $12 in an adjacent lot. The bathrooms have changing tables.

The Chicago Art Institute
111 South Michigan Avenue   www.artic.edu
312-443-3600

The first time I brought my daughter to the Art Institute she was six months old and I purposely left my stroller at home so that we would not take up so much space, and I thought it would give her infant eyes a better view of the art. Big mistake! Backpack carriers are not allowed but they do have strollers available free of charge! Since that visit, I have become a lot smarter about my trips to the Art Institute. There are many aspects of the Art Institute that young children can appreciate. For starters, the "Arms and Armor" collection with all that shiny weaponry makes a big impression on my three-year-old son. The Kraft Education Center has interactive exhibitions and more than 1000 picture books in its collection. The center sponsors family workshops and art activities many weekends. Lastly, admiring the many, many famous works of art is also fun with young children—in a small dose.

Admission is $10 for adults, $6 for children five and older, and the museum is free on Tuesdays. To get on the Kraft Education Center's mailing list call 312-857-7161. You can dine casually in the Court Café. Also, there is a great outdoor area for picnicking, just south of the building, with beautiful low fountains and gardens. Parking is easy at the Grant Park Garage—south entrance. The bathrooms on the lower level have changing tables.

Chicago Children's Museum
Navy Pier   www.chichildrensmuseum.org
700 East Grand Avenue
312-527-1000

The Chicago Children's Museum is a very large space so do not be surprised if you and your child only visit a portion of it each time you go. The museum did a nice job of creating very distinct, separate spaces according to age groups, so there are a couple rooms that my daughter at age seven still has not "graduated" to. There are safe "baby zones" for crawlers in the toddler rooms. Older children love the climbing schooner on which kids can act out their pirate fantasies and test their climbing skills. Also, there is a musical slide that my kids still make a beeline to; a fantastic water room where the kids are certain to get soaked; and in the inventing lab even the youngest tykes can construct their own flying machines.

There is not an eating area within the museum but there are many eating establishments at Navy Pier. The bathrooms are very nice, including small, toddler-size toilets and family bathrooms. Admission is free on Thursday evenings from 5:00 PM to 8:00 PM. The museum is open Tuesday–Sunday, Labor Day through Memorial Day and on Mondays during the summer months and for school holidays throughout the year. Admission is $7 for adults and children (babies under one are free). Memberships are available at different levels with varying benefits. Parking at Navy Pier is very expensive though the museum will validate members' parking tickets, which amounts to a small discount.

Children's Museum of Immigration at the Swedish American Museum Center

5211 North Clark Street www.samac.org
773-728-8111

The Children's Museum of Immigration is great hands-on fun where kids can step back in time to experience what it was like to take the voyage on a boat from Sweden to America—complete with oars to row. Kids can settle into life on a Swedish farm, milk a pretend cow, collect wooden chicken eggs, gather firewood for the stove and prepare a meal for the family. The museum is open Tuesdays–Fridays 1:00 PM–4:00 PM and Saturdays and Sundays 11:00 AM–4:00 PM. Admission is $4 for adults, and $3 for children/senior. The museum offers free admission on the second Tuesday of every month. Street parking is available. The small bathroom is located on the floor below the museum.

DuSable Museum of African American History

740 East 56th Place www.dusablemuseum.org
773-947-0600

The DuSable Museum is most appropriate for school-aged children since it does not have much in the way of interactive exhibits to engage younger children or toddlers. By first grade my daughter had begun to study the Civil Rights Movement and the Underground Railroad so she was able to understand the exhibit on slavery. The museum provides some teachable moments; for example, at the water fountain there is a picture of a fountain from the past depicting a "whites-only" water fountain and a separate, small one for "coloreds." Images such as these are very powerful even for preschool children. Admission is $3 for adults, $1 for children six years and older and free for younger children. Sunday afternoons are free. There is no restaurant inside the museum. A small, free parking lot is available behind the museum and there is free street parking. Bathrooms are equipped with changing tables.

Field Museum of Natural History

1400 South Lake Shore Drive www.fieldmuseum.org
312-922-9410

Known by most kids as the "dinosaur" museum, the Field Museum is a favorite of kids and parents alike. This museum is so huge that in almost seven years of going there we have just begun to scratch the surface. Probably the museum's most famous exhibit is Sue, the largest and most complete Tyrannasorus Rex ever discovered. There are many other dinosaurs to visit along "Dinosaur Hall." One of our favorite exhibits is the "Underground Adventure" where children and adults are "shrunk" to a miniscule size before entering the land of bugs and insects, which now look gigantic – once you are shrunk. Some toddlers may find this exhibit a little scary. We love going on the indoor Nature Walk and walking along a wooden nature trail through various habitats pushing lots of red buttons along the way to hear recordings of various animals and birds. We usually bring our lunch, but there is a Corner Bakery and a McDonalds (that my kids still have not discovered!) in the museum. Admission is $8 for adults and $4 for children (more for non-Chicago residents). Free days are Mondays and Tuesdays for the months of January and February and from September 6th–December 21st. Parking is available in the new indoor garage for $12. The bathrooms on the main floor have changing tables but are small and almost always have a line so plan accordingly. The bathrooms on the lower level are larger and have changing tables.

Hands On! Children's Art Museum
1800 West 103rd Street   www.handsonart.org
773-233-9933

The Hands On! Children's Art Museum is a terrific destination. This museum has everything your child could want to explore and create with. The large open art area of the museum has bin after bin filled with paper, paints, pastels, markers, beads, pom-poms, scissors, fabrics, Popsicle sticks, bottle caps—and more. There is also a room dedicated to creating with clay, including a pottery wheel. Hands On! offers an imagination playroom complete with a castle, dress-up clothes and a puppet theater. There are smaller areas sectioned off for children who want to play with blocks, a tree house, puzzles, legos and more. No food is sold in the museum; there is a changing table in one of the bathrooms and a small parking lot behind the museum. Admittance is $5 per person. The museum also offers great ongoing and one-time classes.

Mexican Fine Arts Center Museum
1852 West 19th Street   www.mfacmchicago.org
312-738-1503

The Mexican Fine Arts Center Museum is the largest Latino cultural institution in the country. It is a beautiful building with a vibrant permanent collection and special exhibits. This museum is definitely geared toward older children with hands-on activities offered only on occasional Sundays and for children ages six and older. However, the permanent collection, which includes paintings, photographs and sculptures, provides a dynamic look at Mexican culture. A great occasion to visit the museum with young children is the "Dia Del Nino Festival," a day of celebrating children. This festival features hands-on art activities, entertainment and prizes and occurs each spring; call for the exact date and time. The museum runs a summer art camp for kids ages five and older. During special exhibits, the museum also sponsors a free family day one Sunday per month between 2:00 PM and 4:00 PM. Call for details. The museum does not have a parking lot but street parking is easy to find and no food is sold within the museum. Admission is free. Bathrooms have changing tables.

The Oriental Institute Museum
1155 East 58th Street   www.oi.uchicago.org
773-702-9514

The Oriental Institute is an awe-inspiring spot for children and parents. It is a relatively small museum with an impressive collection of artifacts that University of Chicago archeologists have excavated throughout the decades. There is a large amount of pottery and tablets that will not necessarily intrigue a young child but there is plenty that will, including mummies, a colossal statue of King Tut and ancient games. The museum is free and open Tuesdays–Sundays. There is ample street parking and no food is sold or allowed in the museum. The bathroom has a changing table.

Peggy Notebaert Nature Museum
2430 North Cannon Drive   www.chias.org
773-755-5111

In our family, this museum is known as the "butterfly museum" for its beautiful 2,700-square-foot glass atrium with more than 50 species of butterflies. Chicago's newest museum, the Notebaert Nature Museum is architecturally striking. It has a spectacular outdoor garden that borders North Pond and is accessible during the warmer months. Notebaert has a great space for toddlers known as "Hands-on Habitat," which includes a two-story tree house, a cave they can explore in animal costume and more. The Butterfly Café is a cafeteria-style eatery and a charming place to enjoy lunch with its beautiful views. Admission is $7 for adults, $4 for children ages 3–12 and $5 for students ages 13–25. Thursday is free day. The museum offers street parking only or paid parking at the adjacent city lot. The museum has large bathrooms with changing tables.

The Museum of Science and Industry
57th Street and Lake Shore Drive   www.msichicago.org
773-684-1414

The Museum of Science and Industry is such an impressive museum. It is also a very accessible museum, especially in the winter as it has an underground parking lot from which you can directly enter the building. There are so many unique exhibits to explore at this museum, from "Flight 727" to the Baby Chicks to the Apollo 8 Command Module to the U-505 Submarine, and much more. A favorite spot for babies and older kids alike is the Idea Factory. Parents will appreciate how thoughtfully designed this place is, with separate age-appropriate sections for babies, toddlers and big kids. The Idea Factory has a lot of water experiments and cause and effect experiments using balls, trucks and blocks. There is a nicely remodeled food court. Admission is $8 for adults and $4.25 for children age 3 to 11 (admission rates are higher for non-Chicago residents). The museum is free on Mondays and Tuesdays during the months of January and February and again from September 13th–November 30th. Parking is $12 if you are not a member. Bathrooms are large and have changing tables.

John G. Shedd Aquarium
1200 South Lake Shore Drive   www.sheddnet.org
312-692-3333

The Shedd Aquarium has experienced fantastic growth in the last few years. The oceanarium, the world's largest indoor marine mammal pavilion features beluga whales and pacific white-sided dolphins. Each day marine mammal trainers host several shows during which dolphins will leap, "walk" on their back fins and perform other natural behaviors on command. The shows are very educational in nature; young toddlers may grow a bit restless but if they can hang on for about five minutes they will be delighted by the simultaneous performances of the dolphins at the conclusion. Do not miss the underwater viewing area where you can see excellent, close views of dolphins diving and whales swimming by. There is a mesmerizing exhibit of sea horses—the highlight for my kids. The latest addition, Wild Reef, features a stunning 12-foot, floor-to-ceiling shark aquarium, containing more than 30 sharks.

The aquarium has a food court and a beautiful dining room overlooking Lake Michigan and a fancier restaurant above the food court. Members receive a 10 percent discount. The aquarium is an expensive outing with adult tickets priced at $14 (more if you're not a Chicago resident) and children's tickets (under three is free) priced at $10 (again, more if you're not a Chicago resident). Shedd has its own version of free days, offering reduced pricing on Mondays and Tuesdays from October through February and free admission on those days to the main building only (not the oceanarium or Wild Reef exhibits). Parking is available in the new indoor garage for $12. Bathrooms are large with changing tables.

Big City Locations

American Girl Place
111 East Chicago Avenue   www.americangirl.com
877-AG-PLACE

Well, there is no place like it. The American Girl Place covers three floors and boasts a theater, restaurant and large retail space. Girls and their families can attend the "Circle of Friends" musical; tickets are $26. Girls also can bring their dolls to the American Girl Café for lunch, tea or dinner. High chairs are provided for the dolls so that "mom" has her hands free to enjoy her meal. There is a preset menu ranging from $16 to $18 per person. Of course there are numerous shopping opportunities, which include the purchase of high-end dolls, their clothes, furniture, toys and accessories. There is also a girls' clothing boutique where girls can select outfits and accessories to match their dolls. Girls can even get their doll's hair styled! To top it all off, your daughter can become a "cover girl" posing for her own American Girl cover for $21.95. No designated parking lot.

Chinatown
Cermack & 22nd Streets

Chinatown can feel a bit like a foreign land for kids who experience this part of the city. It offers different foods, new smells, unique architecture and, of course, a predominately Chinese population. My kids and I like to wander down Wentworth Avenue, the main street, where we venture into the various shops. We purchase and devour a large bag of fortune cookies (for only $2.50) and explore the many shops that sell intriguing items such as miniature dragons, foldable fans and a wealth of Hello Kitty items. My older child also likes Chinese astrology, where you identify the year of what animal you were born in. Throughout Chinatown you can purchase astrology charts or posters. It also is an eye-opening experience to visit the food shops and see the large bins of items for sale, which include dried seahorses! Finally, visit the Chicago Public Library in Chinatown and show your kids a popular book such as "Where the Wild Things Are," in Chinese; even the youngest child can appreciate the unique characters that make up the Chinese alphabet. Your best bathroom option is a restaurant or the library. Street parking is plentiful.

Garfield Park Conservatory

300 North Central Park Boulevard   www.garfield-conservatory.org
312-746-5100

Looking for an escape from Chicago's cold, long, long winters? Grab you baby or toddler and head to the Garfield Conservatory. The gardens are beautiful and offer views of many different habitats including a tropical rainforest, a desert and more. My kids love to walk (o.k., run) along the twisting tree and plant covered paths. In addition, there is a "Children's Garden," complete with a hands-on soil table, a large slide, an oversized seedling to peek into and a giant bee pollinating a flower. Also, the conservatory sponsors many unique and fun activities on Saturdays throughout the year. Admission is free, though special exhibits suggest a $3 donation. There is a free parking lot next to the conservatory. The conservatory has a concession stand where they sell hot dogs, sandwiches, wraps and more. Bathrooms are equipped with changing tables.

Lincoln Park Conservatory

2391 North Stockton Drive
312-742-7736

While dwarfed in size compared to the Garfield Park Conservatory the Lincoln Park Conservatory is a beautiful place to visit in winter or summer. Upon entering the glass-domed structure you are engulfed by the tropical air and the lush environment. It is a transition that is awe striking for even the youngest child. During the warm months the outside gardens are even more spectacular. Children can run among the aisles of beautiful garden beds and make a wish in the large fountain. It is a perfect place to picnic among the beautiful flowers, with Chicago's impressive skyline in the background. When you visit the Lincoln Park Conservatory you cannot help but feel fortunate to live in a city as wonderful as Chicago. Pack your camera, as this is a fabulous place to snap baby's picture and send it to all your friends. Admission is free. Bathrooms are large and have changing tables. There is street parking or paid parking along Cannon Drive (better known as the zoo parking lot) for $12.

Lincoln Park Zoo

2200 North Cannon Drive   www.lpzoo.org
312-742-2000

My children never tire of the Lincoln Park Zoo! The zoo is free (parking on Cannon Drive is $12) and open every day of the year. It is a great zoo for families with young children because you never have to walk too far to see an exhibit. There are many indoor and outdoor exhibits so it's a fun place to visit in the winter too. At the Pritzker Children's Zoo the animals are at toddler eye level and zoo volunteers are on hand to help children pet some of them. The new Regenstein African Journey is fabulous with elephants, giraffes, rhinos and more. Also, the new exhibit is a great winter destination because most of it is indoors. Another favorite is the Endangered Species Carousel, where for $2 children can ride on their favorite endangered animal and get a collector's card.

The newly renovated farm inside the zoo is a delight for young children. At certain times each day children can feed the cows and pet the goats. The farm also has a fantastic, indoor play space with interactive exhibits—another great reason to visit the zoo in the winter! In the summertime you can rent paddleboats and cruise around the lagoon. Strollers and wagons are also available for rent. Although the zoo is free membership is affordable at $60 a year and well worth it because it includes free parking passes. Lastly, the zoo offers great classes for toddlers and older children. There is a very nice food court (with indoor and outdoor eating) and great bathrooms located downstairs. All buildings have bathrooms though the size varies.

Navy Pier
700 East Grand   www.navypier.com
312-595-PIER

Navy Pier is a choice destination spot for Chicago families and tourists alike. In addition to the Chicago Children's Museum's home, Navy Pier also offers an IMAX theater, miniature golf, a carousel, a giant ferris wheel, a free climbing wall and a swing ride—and that just covers the amusement activities (most rides are between $3 and $5 for children). Numerous boat tour companies are docked at Navy Pier. This is an expensive endeavor but worth it at least once. Other activities include a 3D Ride and a giant maze—both for a fee. A day at Navy Pier adds up with the activities, parking and food. Fortunately there are some nice "freebies," such as the roving entertainers, which include singers, magicians, jugglers and more. The Crystal Garden is another nice and free destination that features unique water-jumping fountains that my kids love to run under. Navy Pier has a fabulous outdoor water fountain that kids can play and jump in on hot summer days. A word of caution, Navy Pier hosts frequent well-attended expositions so before you go (especially on a weekend) call ahead and find out what is happening that day. The pier has large bathrooms with changing tables.

John Hancock
875 North Michigan Avenue   www.hancock-observatory.com
888-875-VIEW

Show your kids how they can view four states from one spot when you visit the John Hancock Observatory. On a clear day it's a fun place to venture with kids. Aside from the spectacular view there are computerized games and a place where kids can pretend to be window washers on a skyscraper. I find it helpful to visit with another adult. The lines to ride the elevator back down can be long so it's best to have one adult occupy the kids while the other one holds a place in line. It costs $9.50 for adults, children four years and younger are free and older children are $4. Paid parking is available in the building and is accessible from Chestnut and Delaware Streets.

Sears Tower Skydeck
233 South Wacker Drive   www.sears-tower.com
312-875-9696

If the view from John Hancock is not high enough for your kids, you can try the Sears Tower Skydeck, which is several floors higher. Sears Tower Skydeck has kid-friendly displays called "Knee-High Chicago." The cutout windows provide interesting images and facts about Chicago in kid-friendly terms. The most exciting part of your visit will undoubtedly be the elevators where you feel like you are blasting off through the top of the Sears Tower and into space—with views of the earth compliments of NASA and the Space Shuttle Endeavor! This atmosphere is made possible via 50-inch flat screen monitors that are mounted in the elevators. Admission is $9.95 for adults, free for children under age three and $6.95 for kids age 3 to 11. There is a designated parking lot across the street from the Sear's Tower.

Libraries

The Chicago Public Libraries are a treasure and a great resource for parents and young children. With 79 locations throughout the city most families do not have to venture too far to find a neighborhood library. While there are too many libraries to list in this book, here are some that have large children's sections. Most of these locations also have parking lots. Also, many of these libraries have fun story times divided by age and include babies, toddlers and preschoolers. To get a complete list of libraries go to the Web site at www.chipublib.org. The Web site is fairly user friendly. Click on "programs for children" to find listings by date and location of special children's events; unfortunately, it does not give you the individual story times for each branch. Also, on the Web site you will find details about each library, such as hours of operation, location and CTA service information.

Thomas Hughes Children's Library
Harold Washington
400 South State Street
312-747–4647

Blackstone Branch
4904 South Lake Park Avenue
312-747-0511

Edgebrook Branch
5331 West Devon
312-744-8313

Edgewater Branch
1210 West Elmdale
312-744-0718

John Merlo Branch
644 West Belmont
312-744-1139

Lincoln Belmont Branch
1659 West Melrose
312-744-0166

Lincoln Park Branch
1150 West Fullerton
312-744-1926

Logan Square Branch
3255 West Altgeld
312-744-5295

Near North Branch
310 West Division
312-744-0991

Suzler Regional Library
4455 North Lincoln Avenue
312-744-7616

Uptown Branch
929 West Buena
312-744-8400

Theater & Musical Events

The Chicago Chamber Musicians
Annual Family Concert   www.chicagochambermusic.org
Chicago Shakespeare Theater on Navy Pier
800 East Grand Avenue
312-595-5600

This fabulous annual event sets children's favorite stories to music. The event is held only one weekend a year, usually in January. Two showings per day are offered on Saturday and Sunday. Tickets sell out so get on the mailing list. These shows are appropriate for children three and older, though my son went to the *Peter and the Wolf* show when he was 22 months old and loved it. Parking at Navy Pier is expensive; the theater has large, nice bathrooms.

Emerald City Theatre Company
The Apollo Theater   www.emeraldcitytheatre.com
2540 North Lincoln Avenue
773-529-2690

Season tickets to this theatre company are a must for every family. Emerald City Theatre produces four engaging and unique shows a year based on popular fairy tales and children's stories. The company includes recommended ages for each show in its program descriptions. Season tickets are $30.50 for children and $40 for adults. Tickets for individual performances are also sold. Paid parking is available in the adjacent lot. The theater has small bathrooms.

Kraft Family Matinee Series
Chicago Symphony Orchestra   www.cso.org
220 South Michigan Avenue
312-294-3000

Kraft Family Matinee Series is a great way to introduce young children to music. It is a thrilling experience to go to beautiful Symphony Center. These series are recommended for children ages five and older but many families bring younger children to the concerts. The event typically combines the experience of listening to music with a presentation on how different types of music are created. Children who attend the series must be old enough to sit for periods of time during which an adult is talking lecture-style. Call for prices and a schedule. Parking is available in the Grant Street Garage—South. The bathrooms do not have changing tables.

Lifeline Theatre
6912 North Glenwood   www.lifelinetheatre.com
773-761-4477

Lifeline Theatre has wonderfully funny and creative shows that uniquely adapt favorite children's books. The plays are based on classics and newer books; one of their biggest recent hits was adapted from the book *Click Clack Moo: Cows That Type.* All seats are $8. The theatre offers student matinee shows, midweek, for the discounted fee of $6. Street parking is available or paid parking in a nearby lot. The theatre has a small bathroom.

Second City Children's Theatre
1616 Wells Street   www.secondcity.com
312-377-3992

Second City developed a hilarious children's theatre program that works within the parameters of favorite children's stories. The Second City format is interactive. Kids participate in the narration of each story. Paid parking is available in the attached garage. Kid-friendly drinks are sold at the theatre. The theatre has a small bathroom.

Drop-In Hot Spots

Corner Playroom
2121 North Clybourn   www.cornerplayroom.com
773-388-2121

The Corner Playroom is exactly what the stay-at-home mom, who is tired of sitting in her own playroom all Chicago-winter-and-spring, would order up if she could. It accommodates kids ages six months to five years. The playroom features colorful walls with whimsical paintings, large playhouses and climbing toys. It has a smaller room for quieter activities such as puzzles and books. Snacks are available for a fee. The Corner Playroom offers one- to three-month memberships ranging from $85 to $165. Once you are a member, you can go anytime during the hours of 9:00 AM to 5:30 PM. Friday afternoons, Saturdays and Sundays are reserved for parties. The Corner Playroom offers art and music classes for additional fees ($135 for a 10-week session). A nice bonus is that the Corner Playroom is located in a shopping mall with free parking. Drop-off summer camps are offered too. Free parking in the attached lot.

Fantasy Kingdom
1418 North Kingsbury Street
312-642-KIDS

Fantasy Kingdom is a thrilling drop-in play space for children ages six months through six years. Your child can act out his knightly fantasies in a castle, which is 30 feet wide and 10 feet high. Adventuresome princes and princesses can scale the attached climbing wall and/or whoosh down the slide. If your child would prefer to play the role of a "commoner" she can explore the "village," which includes a market, a fire station, a police station and a pink Tudor house. Each "building" offers dress up clothes and props to complete the fantasy play. Young babies and toddlers can play safely with toys in a space that is separated by a partial wall from the rest of the room. There is an open eating area accessible to families looking for a spot to enjoy a snack. Prepackaged snack items are sold at Fantasy Kingdom or families can bring their own. Fantasy Kingdom shares space in a large building, along the industrial corridor on Kingsbury Street. The bathrooms are located in the public space outside of the play area and include changing tables. Parking is available in the attached garage. Daily admission is $10 per child (siblings less than one year are admitted for free). Discounted rates are available in one-, three- and six-month packages. Fantasy Kingdom can be rented for birthday parties on the weekends. It is open to the public Monday–Friday from 9:30 AM–5:30 PM.

Thursday Afternoon Drop-In
New City YMCA, 'Mazing Kids Room
1515 North Halsted
312-440-1203

Each Thursday, from 1:30 to 3:00 PM parents gather with child development specialist Karen Benson to chat informally while the children play. The 'Mazing Kids Room is an energy-charged playroom complete with climbing equipment, make believe toys and even computer games for older kids. It is one of the few places where families can take their infants, toddlers and preschool-aged children. It provides a nice break from our long, Chicago winters. Cost is $5 per family (sliding scale available). Free parking is available in the attached parking lot.

Toddlers' Playhouse
Located in the Broadway United Methodist Church
3344 North Broadway
773-529-4740

Toddlers' Playhouse is a fun place for children ages six months to three years to play with a caregiver. It offers a large indoors play space where kids can climb on play structures, gas up and drive pretend cars, play house complete with dress-up clothes and have a snack. Designed to help hedge off the isolation of a Chicago winter, families can enroll for a 15-week fall/early winter session or winter/spring session; the cost is $180 a session. Street parking.

Dining Out

Like many Chicagoans dining out is one of my favorite past times. Now that I have children I do not get to enjoy leisurely meals out nearly as often as I used to. But being a parent doesn't mean your dining out days are behind you, rather you just need to find the right place and adopt the right frame of mind. In general, family friendly restaurants have a children's menu, employ friendly wait staff, offer speedy service, provide changing tables and ideally, hand out some type of activity for children while you wait for your meal. In a city the size of Chicago there are many family friendly restaurants. Below is a list of some of my favorite spots for eating out with tots.

Ben & Jerry's
338 West Armitage Avenue
773-281-3150

26 West Randolph Street
312-252-2900
Other locations throughout the city

It's Ben & Jerry's ice cream, what more needs to be said! This is a fun and delicious spot to indulge your and your child's sweet tooth. There is a small bathroom and street parking at the Armitage location.

Make a special trip to Ben & Jerry's in the Loop to support the Choir Academy of the Chicago Children's Choir, a non-profit organization. Ben & Jerry's has created "PartnerShops," which are owned and operated by non-profits to create a place where young people can gain job and entrepreneurial skills and the revenues help support vital community organizations. No specific parking garage for the Loop location.

Box Car Cafe
723 West Wrightwood Avenue   www.boxcarcafe.net
773-325-9560

Box Car Café is made for hanging out with kids. As you can guess by the name, a train theme runs throughout the café. My son loves to see his drink delivered by a train that runs along a track (just above kid-head-level) from the kitchen to the dining area. The menu features kid favorites such as hot dogs and grilled cheese for $2.99. They also offer tempting sandwiches for adults. Parents can buy any kind of coffee drink desired and kids are set, winter or summer, with hot chocolate or ice cream. In addition to large train murals and old trains on display, there is a toy box, crayons and paper and kid-size tables. The café has street parking and a tiny, tiny bathroom.

Brasserie Jo
59 West Hubbard Street
312-595-0800

Brasserie Jo is a great place to go if you desire a more upscale dining experience that is also kid-friendly. Upon arriving, children receive a child's menu that is attached to an etch-a-sketch for them to play with. The menu covers all the bases; for the picky eater there is grilled cheese and pasta. For children with a more sophisticated taste, Brasserie Jo offers a tomato tarte and cheese with pommes frites, chicken escalope and salmon. The best part is that kids do not even have to clean their plates to get dessert because a serving of petite chocolate mousse comes with every meal. The menu also shows kids how to count to 12 in French. Bon appetite! The bathrooms have changing tables. Valet parking is available.

Café Selmarie
4729 North Lincoln Avenue
773-989-5595

While Café Selmarie does not have a separate children's menu it does provide a child's portion size of pasta or child's pizza. It is a very fun place to dine with children especially in the summer when the restaurant fills the plaza of Lincoln Square with its tables. Children love to dine here because they can run around and chase the pigeons or throw pennies in the fountain while parents eat. The restaurant also has a bakery so there are plenty of tasty treats for the family. Bathrooms do not have changing tables. Street parking.

Charlie's Ale House
1224 West Webster Avenue
773-871-1440

5308 North Clark Street
773-751-0140

Charlie's Ale House has burgers, chicken tenders, grilled cheese and noodles—all for $5. Kids are given crayons to keep them entertained while they wait. Street parking only for both locations, though if going to the Andersonville location you can park in the bank parking lot (just 1 block north) if it is after hours. Bathrooms at both locations have changing tables.

Ed Debevic's
640 North Wells Street
312-664-1707

Kids love this restaurant where the wait staff are obnoxious and silly. The wait staff spontaneously launch into song and dance, jump onto countertops and sit down at your table for a friendly chat. The menu is a hit with kids and includes cheeseburgers, hot dogs, chicken fingers and grilled cheese all for $5.99. The best part is the kiddie-dessert, which is a miniature ice cream sundae (think egg cup). Kids are delighted with the sundae and so are parents because it is just the right amount of dessert. Bathrooms have changing tables. Valet parking is available in their attached parking lot.

Edgebrook Coffee Shop & Diner
6322 North Central Avenue
773-792-1433

When you walk into Edgebrook Coffee Shop & Diner it's like stepping back in time about four decades. The diner provides counter service only (no highchairs) and serves diner standbys such as tuna melts, grilled cheese sandwiches and breakfast all day long, including chocolate chip pancakes! Desserts are homemade and the milkshakes are extra thick. The diner is developing a children's menu but they can accommodate the typical kid request. The bathrooms do not have changing tables. Parking is easy on the street or behind the restaurant in the lot.

Goose Island Brew Pub
1800 North Clybourn   www.gooseisland.com
312-915-0071

Goose Island Brew Pub is a very family friendly restaurant. The wait staff is very good with children and the menu features all the kid favorites, such as mac & cheese, fish sticks, chicken fingers, quesadillas, and more. Kids get crayons, miniature books to draw in and toy games. Bathrooms do not have changing tables. The attached parking lot is convenient.

GP Franklin's
4767 North Lincoln Avenue
773-293-1900

www.gpfranklins.com

Franklin's is a festive new restaurant for the entire family. Located in charming Lincoln Square, the restaurant boasts an old fashioned soda fountain—serving homemade ice cream, an intriguing "mountain" that children can climb through and a large sit-down restaurant. The kid's menu is packed with favorites, including mac & cheese, pasta, grilled cheese, chicken nuggets and corn dogs, all for $4.95. My daughter's favorite is the "make your own pizza," in which the ingredients are brought to the table and the child puts the pizza together. Adults will find many tasty favorites on the menu. There are casual dining options such as sandwiches and burgers. Those wanting a heartier meal can select from the "Just Like Sunday At Grandma's" portion of the menu that features favorites such as pork chops, meatloaf and fried chicken. Beer and wine are served.

The "mountain" display will occupy kids while waiting for the meal to be served. It includes a chocolate exploding volcano, miniature trains, gondolas, castles and more. Franklin's also serves breakfast. Lastly, Franklin's is a fantastic spot for a birthday party. It offers a private party room and a great selection of entertainment (provided by The Old Town School of Folk Music), including *Wiggleworms,* or art parties, clowns, magicians and much more. Parking is available along Lincoln Square or just south of the restaurant in a metered parking lot. Bathrooms provide changing table.

John's Place
1202 West Webster Avenue
773-525-6670

Families flock here! A park and playground across the street add to the draw. John's Place is extremely family friendly. Kiddies enjoy the typical kid menu of pasta, grilled cheese, mac & cheese, chicken hot dogs and dino bites (chicken). Kids also delight in the smoothies or milkshakes. John's Place is particularly popular in the summer months when families crowd the sidewalks to dine outside. Bathrooms have changing tables. Street parking only.

Kitsch'n on Roscoe
2005 West Roscoe Street
773-248-7372

A big hit with kids and parents alike, Kitsch'n is an easy restaurant to enjoy. The kid's menu is yummy and fun and at $4 for lunch or dinner, and breakfasts from $1 to $3.50, it is a real bargain. My kids' favorite is "Sean's retro lunch box," consisting of a grilled cheese or PJB sandwich, with the crust cut-off (of course) and a choice of a Twinkie or Ding Dong served in a retro metal school lunch box—think Wonder Woman and G.I. Joe. An outdoor patio and tasty adult meals make for a happy family outing. One bathroom has a changing table. Street parking.

Margies Candies
1960 North Western Avenue
773-384-1035

Margie's Candies is an institution in Chicago, serving terrific ice cream sundaes and candy treats since 1921. Prepare yourself, the ice cream sundaes are huge and the menu features three pages of ice cream selections! The restaurant also has sandwiches, hot dogs, hamburgers and more. There is one extremely small bathroom that I would like to see you try and change a diaper in! Street parking only.

Medici
1237 East 57th Street
773-667-7394

Medici has a great children's menu that features kid favorites such as spaghetti, grilled cheese, pizza, chicken fingers and hamburgers, all for $3 to $3.75. It also has kid's milk shakes and San Francisco's Ghirardelli Hot Chocolate—a big hit! Grown-ups also will find plenty to enjoy on this casual and extensive menu. The bathrooms do not have changing tables. Street parking.

Pauline's
1754 West Balmoral
773-561-8573

Pauline's is a great breakfast and lunch spot (it closes at 3:00 PM) It is an especially fun summer spot with outdoor tables. The atmosphere is homey yet eclectic. The food is fantastic and the portions are humongous. Pauline's doesn't have a separate children's menu but it can accommodate children's smaller appetites by splitting orders. A big hit with the kiddies is the chocolate chip pancakes. The restaurant also serves ice cream and terrific homemade lemon aid. There is ample street parking; no changing tables in the tiny bathroom.

Southport Grocery and Café
3552 North Southport   www.southportgrocery.com
773-665-0100

Southport Grocery and Café was voted most kid-friendly place of the year by Bon Appetite magazine in 2003. It is a stylish and delicious grocery store and café. The store sells high-end, gourmet items and the restaurant is open for breakfast, lunch and an early dinner (closing at 7:00 PM, earlier on weekends). The children's menu offers all items for $4 and includes bread pudding pancakes, eggs and French toast for breakfast, and grilled cheese, buttered noodles and PB&J for lunch and dinner. No changing tables in the bathroom but there is ample room to change baby on the floor.

SuperDawg
Milwaukee at Devon and Nagel
773-478-7800

Located on the far northwest corner of the city you will find an authentic drive-up restaurant. My kids never cease to be amazed by this old-fashioned drive-up where we push a button to order our food, which is then delivered to our car complete with a tray that hooks onto our car window! In addition to the thrill of the drive-up, the food is tasty and includes American favorites such as hotdogs, grilled cheese, hamburgers and thick milkshakes. You cannot miss this place, just look for the giant his and her hotdogs on top of the building. The restaurant has bathrooms.

Sweet Mandy B's
1208 West Webster Place
773-244-1174

There is no place sweeter than Sweet Mandy B's. This is one of my kids (and my) favorite destinations and I am embarrassed to say we go almost weekly for a treat. If you could dream up a sweet shop this would be it! Decorated in cheerful yellow and blues it has an eat-on counter top complete with spinning stools. Mandy B's offers the yummiest cupcakes and numerous other tasty treats, such as cookies, whoopee pies, chocolate and banana pudding . . . I could go on and on. The restaurant has two bathrooms, (with changing tables) which are great for cleaning up gooey kids. Sweet Many B's is just steps away from John's Place, which makes it the perfect dessert stop after dinner. Street parking.

Sweet Occasions
4639 North Damen Avenue   www.sweetoccasionsandmore.com
773-293-3080

1622 West Morse Avenue
773-262-0880

*An Uptown location will open Summer 2004

Sweet Occasions delights children and parents alike with its candy-filled bins, 110 ice cream flavors, scrumptious desserts and gourmet sandwiches. It is a festive and delicious treat! It also specializes in candy gift baskets. Sweet Occasions is a great place for a birthday party. Bathrooms do not have changing tables. Street parking only at each location.

Wishbone Restaurant
3300 North Lincoln Avenue
773-549-2663

1001 West Washington Boulevard
312-850-2663

Wishbone is a major tot hot spot in Chicago. Every time we dine at Wishbone, morning or night, we are in good family company. The menu is southern-styled and there is a separate children's menu that features chicken, burgers, mac & cheese and grilled cheese for lunch or dinner, all for less than $5. Wishbone also is a great breakfast spot. It serves eggs, French toast, pancakes and more for $3 to $3.50. Crayons and coloring sheets are a staple and the service is fast and very friendly. Street parking only. Wishbone has bathrooms with changing tables.

Chapter 7

Sign Me Up! Classes for Babies, Toddlers & Preschoolers

~ Catchalls ~ Music ~ Dance ~ Art ~ Theater ~ Foreign Language

There is no shortage of stimulating and fun classes for you and your baby, toddler or preschooler in Chicago. When I was co-director of the Northside Parents Network, I often fielded calls from panicked parents whose two- or three-year-olds did not get into a preschool. One of the first suggestions I offered to these parents was that in a city like Chicago you can piece together a rich and engaging experience for your child whether or not he or she is in preschool. The selection of art, music, dance and foreign language classes listed below is immense. (Physical play classes and sport programs are described in Chapter 8.)

My children and I participated in or visited almost every program listed. While all the programs included are high quality, they are not for every child. For example, I am having a very different "class experience" with my son than with my daughter. My daughter could happily participate in any class because she is outgoing and eager to gain independence. My son prefers to stay home but when he does venture out he enjoys classes that are unstructured. So word to the wise, think about your child's personality when selecting classes and resist the urge to try everything at once!

The classes described in this section are divided into categories. Categories include music, dance, art, theater, foreign language and a category I term "catchalls," to describe organizations that offer a wide breadth of children's programming. You will note that some organizations are listed in more than one category because they offer more than one type of class. Also, organizations are listed alphabetically.

Catchalls

The organizations listed below offer such a wealth of quality classes across many different categories that it would be repetitive to list them each time. So check out these one-stop-shopping organizations. They are certain to meet your child's ever-changing interest.

The Beverly Arts Center
2407 West 111th Street   www.beverlyartcenter.org
773-445-3838
Ages 2 and up

The Beverly Arts Center offers an impressive line up of art classes. Children ages two and three take classes along with mom, dad or a caregiver and get to explore in clay, paint and other mediums. Older children take classes independently and choose from a range of classes that allow them to explore many different mediums from watercolor to charcoal to paints. The center offers monthly family workshops on Saturday afternoons. Classes are 10 weeks and cost between $100 and $180. The Beverly Arts Center also houses the Lou Conte Dance Studio. Classes are available for children five years and older and include creative movement and ballet. Ten-week sessions begin at $144. Finally, the Beverly Arts Center provides a Suzuki music program taught by the Sherwood Conservatory of Music. Classes begin for children ages four and older. Call for specifics. There is plenty of free parking and in the late afternoon a small café serves light food.

Bubbles Academy
1504 North Fremont   www.bubblesacademy.com
312-944-7677
Ages infant to 5 years

Bubbles Academy elicits a gasp immediately upon entering. This huge space contains an immense hand-painted mural designed to give (the large studio) an open-field feeling. It is especially well suited for babies because the studio is covered with plush carpeting. Bubbles offers two types of music classes for infants and crawlers and a separate program for walkers through children age five. There are imagination classes for three- to five-year-olds where children hear stories, sing songs and play theater games. Finally, Bubbles Academy offers yoga classes beginning at age one.

Bubbles Academy provides a separate parent/caregiver observation area complete with comfy seating and coffee. There is a play center where siblings are entertained while mom or dad accompanies their other child to a class. The play center costs $6 an hour. Classes are $140 for an 8-week session. Parking is available in a parking lot across the street for $2. Bubbles Academy is a great, albeit expensive, place for birthday parties.

Chicago Park District

312-742-PLAY   www.chicagoparkdistrict.com

Ages newborn and up

If you're reading this book and already have a child, there's little doubt that you've discovered your neighborhood park district. We Chicagoans are fortunate to have wonderful park districts that offer a wide range of programming at bargain prices. If you've not taken a class with your child it is an excellent place to get started. Most of the park district classes are low key, which makes it a great way to socialize with your child and make mommy friends. At $25 you will never feel guilty if you miss one.

The exact classes and programs vary within each park district. Some of the programs offered include "Mom, Pop and Tot," arts-and-crafts, dance, theater, preschool, holiday events including daddy/daughter and mother/son dances and so much more. (See Chapter 8 for more details about sports programming.) The wealth of programming is stunning.

To learn more about Chicago Park District's programs visit their user-friendly Web site. This Web site lets you search for programs based on park district name, zip code, key word, program or age group. Registration for classes is four times a year in conjunction with the changing of the seasons. Registration recently became easier since the park district now sets aside a certain portion of the spaces for registration online. One caution, in the past, the server has crashed due to the demand. However, if you have ever gotten up at 4:00 AM to get in line to register your child for one of these programs you can appreciate my enthusiasm for this improvement.

Hyde Park Jewish Community Center (JCC)

5200 South Hyde Park Boulevard   www.goJCC.org

773-753-3080

Ages infants and up

The Hyde Park JCC is a beautiful, modern facility with an attached parking lot. The center provides a range of programs that include music and movement classes for infants and their parents/caregivers. For preschoolers and older children it offers art, music, cooking, science, Spanish and drama classes. Hyde Park JCC has a terrific sports program (see Chapter 8 for details). Lastly, Hyde Park JCC sponsors a drop-in, open gym program during the winter months on Tuesdays and Thursdays from 9:15 AM to 11:00 AM at the bargain price of $35 for the entire season.

Menomonee Club

224 West Willow Street
312-664-4631

Drucker Center
1535 North Dayton Street
Ages pre-kindergarten to 6th grade

www.menomoneeclub.org

Menomonee Club is a terrific place for kids ages four and older and is widely popular with both kids and parents. It provides a wide range of programs that include an extensive sports program (see Chapter 8). Menomonee Club offers many dance classes, such as creative movement, hip-hop, Jazz, modern dance and tap. Kids also can participate in brownies or scouts, drama, a variety of art classes, magic, cooking, chess and more. A parent favorite is the Clubhouse Friday Night Movies during which kids watch a movie and hang out while parents have a couple hours to themselves. There is also a game room and open gym times for members. Membership is $60/child/year and reduced rates for classes are available to members. The price for classes varies significantly depending on the length of the program and the activity. In general, prices range from $150 to $255. Street parking for the Willow Street location. The Drucker Center has a parking lot.

Old Town School of Folk Music

Lincoln Park location
909 West Armitage
773-728-6000

www.oldtownschool.org

Lincoln Square location
4544 North Lincoln
773-728-6000

Some classes are offered in the suburbs
Ages infant and up

Probably best known for its children's music class, *Wiggleworms*, Old Town School of Folk Music has a wealth of children's programming. Their classes include music, dance, art and theater. Old Town's music program is extensive. Babies and their parents can participate in *Wiggleworms*, a class so popular it has become a rite of passage for families in Chicago. *Wiggleworms* is offered in English, Spanish, French and German, from infancy through age three. Classes are $105 for an 8-week session. Old Town also offers group lessons for violin, drums, cello, piano, guitar, Irish fiddle and more. Private lessons are also available for $170 for an 8-week session.

Old Town has an impressive array of dance classes that include ballet, salsa dancing, tap, Mexican Zapateado, Jazz, Hip-Hop, West African dance and Irish Stepdancing. For the youngest dancers Old Town offers "Kangaroos," where parents join their child for a movement class. Preschoolers graduate to "Jitterbugs" and they get to explore creative movement independently from parents. These classes are available for children ages two to 12 years. An 8-week session is $105.

The Old Town School of Folk Music expanded its programming to include art classes. For two-year-olds, Old Town offers Scribble, a class where parents or caregivers and their child explore paint, clay, glue and much more. Teachers are excellent and very creative. You will be so thankful your kid can have this experience in a classroom and not in your home! Beginning at age three, children attend classes without an adult. Class fees range from $115 to $150 for an 8-week session.

Lastly, Old Town offers a range of theater classes sure to spark and expand your child's imagination. Most theater classes conclude with children getting their first stage performance experience. Classes are either 8 or 16 weeks long and range in price from $105 to $300. These programs are available for children ages three to 16 years.

Parking is difficult at the Armitage location, with street parking your only option. The Lincoln Avenue location has a paid parking lot and street parking is somewhat easier to come by. Both locations offer a snack bar.

Portage Park Center for the Arts
5801 West Dakin Street
773-205-0151
Ages newborns and older

The Portage Park Center for the Arts is one of my greatest finds! The center is Executive Director Jennifer La Civita's brainchild. La Civita successfully created a place where families join together to play and enjoy the arts in a fun and nurturing environment. The range of programs offered is impressive and ever-changing depending on the needs of families.

Creativity Corner is a parent/child class for children two and older. In this class children explore the creative process using art books, art games, puzzles, music and more. Other programs offered include Kindermusik classes for newborns through five-year-olds, Spanish classes, yoga (including yoga for infants and children with special needs), infant/child CPR, Monart drawing classes, mother/daughter belly dancing, cooking, piano lessons, a children's chorus, theatre, nature enrichment classes, workshops and much more. Older children and teenagers will enjoy jewelry making, papier-mâché, watercolor and more.

Class fees vary depending on the program but are very reasonable. Street parking is easy.

YMCA
Ages newborn and up   www.ymcachgo.org

Chicago has many YMCA branches throughout the city and suburbs. While the classes vary depending on each of the branches, many have superb early childhood programs. Four YMCAs that offer a wide range of children's programs include the Lake View, Irving Park, New City and the South Side Y. For specific details call the Y you are interested in. But to give you an idea of the breadth of programs offered at the YMCAs, I have listed below some of their information.

Irving Park YMCA
4251 West Irving Park Road
773-777-7500

Lakeview YMCA
3333 North Marshfield Avenue   www.lakeviewymca.org
773-248-3333

New City YMCA
1515 North Halsted
312-440-7272

South Side YMCA
6330 South Stony Island
773-947-0700

If you are looking for a place for your baby or child to have fun while you exercise check out the Ys "Mazing Kids" rooms (at the Lakeview and New City locations), which offer a variety of activities for children six months–12 years. There is a large climbing area, toys, video games and more.

Most of the Ys listed above offer classes such as infant massage, music, dance and art, (see Chapter 8 for information about their sports programs). Every Friday night the Ys host "Family Night," in which there is open swim and gym playtime. The Ys offer a very popular summer camp program for children ages 3–12 years, preschool programs and after school care. Prices vary depending on whether or not you are a member of the Y; for example, the Junior Picassos art class is $45 for members and $90 for non-members. Prices also vary for each class. Call for details. Each Y has a parking lot.

Music

DePaul Community Music Program
804 West Belden, Room 328   www.music.depaul.edu
773-325-7262
Ages 18 months and up

The DePaul Community Music Program offers a range of music classes that include Kindermusik, Suzuki instruction and traditional individual instruction. Yearly parking lot passes are available for $20, for classes taking place after 3:00 PM—otherwise it is street parking only. For more information about their program see the specific sections on Kindermusik and Suzuki.

Gold Coast Music School
1137 North State Street
312-587-0159
Ages 3 months and up

Gold Coast Music School offers traditional music instruction for a variety of instruments. The school also has a Suzuki and a Kindermusik program (please see Suzuki and Kindermusik sections). All teachers have master's degrees in music. Classes are $30 for 30 minutes of instruction. Street parking.

Gymboree Play & Music
3158 North Lincoln Avenue   www.gymboree.com
773-296-4550
Ages 6 months to 4 years

Gymboree's music program offers high-energy classes that encourage children to sing, dance, listen and create their own music using a variety of different instruments. Classes are offered in 12-week sessions for $195. A one-time only enrollment fee of $25 is required. Children enrolled in a Gymboree class are eligible to participate in open gym play where they can climb, run, jump and have fun in its fabulous facility. Open gym is offered at specific times throughout the week, call for details. Street parking.

Krivoy
1145 West Webster Avenue
773-248-1466
Ages 4 months to 5 years

Once a clothing store, designer and owner Cynthia Hadesman converted her space into a charming and open studio that offers music classes for toddlers and preschoolers. Music instructor Jared Metzger teaches the "BabyBoom" class for one through three-year-olds. In this class toddlers and their caregivers sing, use movement and instruments, such as shaker eggs and adorable beanbags, handmade by Cynthia. Jared offers a mixture of children's songs that mom or dad will recognize and songs he has written to introduce the concepts of beat and melody. Preschoolers will enjoy "RythmMakers," a music class in which they can participate independently. This class is designed to bridge the gap between baby music classes and private lessons in specific instruments. Through movement and simple instruments Jared begins to introduce rhythms and pitch. Jared also provides private instruction in piano and voice. Classes are $120 for the toddler class and $160 for the preschool class for an 8-week session.

Krivoy is also home to "Happy Child Music" and "Happy Family Music," programs developed by Julie Frost. Julie is a Parent's Choice award winning producer of children's music. Her classes are offered for children four months and older. The "Happy Family Music" program is a real lifesaver because it allows children as young as four months to participate and bring along their big sister or brother. Classes begin at $106 and go up to $194 for the family music class for an 8-week session. Julie also teaches a number of different yoga classes for children beginning at age three. Call for a schedule.

Lastly, Cynthia sells a select number of her beautiful handmade children's clothing, including children's cashmere sweaters made from pieces of old sweaters. Street parking.

Malia's Music Studio
3644 North Greenview
773-230-0168
Ages newborn and up

www.maliamusic.info

Malia's Music Studio provides piano instruction in small group settings of three or four kids beginning at age four. The classes include movement in addition to piano instruction. Malia also offers the Kindermusik program for newborns through age four.

Merry Music Makers
Two locations:
Andersonville
Radiance Yoga
5412 North Clark Street

Edgebrook
Dance Academy
5349 West Devon
773-209-8083
Ages newborn to 4 years

Merry Music Makers offers Music Together, a nationally recognized early childhood music education program created by the Center for Music and Young Children in 1985. Each child participates at her/his own level. Children sing, move, chant, listen and explore musical instruments. Parents or caregivers actively participate with their children as they learn about primary music development. Music Together classes are a relaxed, playful and exploratory musical experience. Families receive a CD, cassette and songbook for each semester's unique collection of songs. Classes are offered in 10-week and 12-week sessions for $140–$170. A free demonstration class is available. Street parking.

Musical Magic
2255 West Roscoe
773-529-5600
Ages newborn to 4 years

www.musicalmagic.net

What differentiates Musical Magic from other music programs is that it is a parent/child program cranked up a few notches. Musical Magic is a cheerful and energizing environment where children and parents sing, play with instruments and dance to both popular music and the usual kiddie songs. Other fun elements include a bubble machine that really excites the kids and a parachute with light balls on it that the kids can make jump around. In the warmer months kids conclude the class by going on a brief, outdoor musical parade. Another nice touch, the entire place has hand painted murals. One wall is done in black, white and gray so that the youngest infant can make out the shapes. Finally, Musical Magic offers that highly desirable but hard to find "all ages class" so that you can take both of your kids to one class—ahh! An 11-week class is $187. Street parking.

Kindermusik

Kindermusik is a curriculum-based, educationally focused music program for children ages newborn through seven. Every activity has a "foundation of learning" (FOL) and at-home activities. The program provides creative ways to bring music into your child's life. The curriculum is broken down by age groups; newborn–18 months; 18 months–3 years; three- and four-year-olds; and older. Kindermusik classes are offered at a number of places in Chicago and are similarly prices. Typically, an 8-week session is $150. Below, I have listed some of the schools that provide Kindermusik programs.

DePaul Community Music Program
804 West Belden, Room 328   www.music.depaul.edu
773-325-7262
Ages 18 months to 7 years

Parking passes for the parking lot are available for classes that take place after 3:00 PM for $20 a year. Street parking.

Gold Coast Music School
1137 North State Street
312-587-0159
Ages 3 months to 5 years
Street parking.

Malia's Music Studio
3644 North Greenview   www.maliamusic.info
773-230-0168
Ages newborn to 4 years
Street parking.

Portage Park Center for the Arts
5801 West Dakin Street
Leah Egan 773-637-9936
Ages newborn to 7 years
Street parking.

Suzuki Music School of Lincoln Park
1753 North Fern Court
312-266-9587
Ages newborn to 5 years

Kindermusik classes are taught at the Church of the Three Crosses, 333 West Wisconsin. Street parking.

Sweet Pea's Studio
3717 North Ravenswood   www.sweetpeasstudio.com
Suite 213
773-248-YOGA
Ages newborn to 18 months
Street parking.

Sherwood Conservatory of Music
1312 South Michigan Avenue   www.sherwoodmusic.org
312-427-6267
Ages newborn to 12 years

With an award-winning staff, Sherwood Conservatory offers group classes for parents and children and preschoolers as well as individual lessons. Sherwood provides instruction in traditional and the Suzuki methods (please see Suzuki section). For babies and their parents Sherwood offers "Music Together," a program that uses movement and songs to introduce little ones to the world of music. This class is $165 a session. For children ages four to six years it offers "Soundscapes," where kids learn basic music skills and "Percussion for Kids," where they make music and explore rhythms. Parking is available in a paid lot a half block south of the school or street parking.

Sing n' Dance
2632 North Halsted   www.singndance.com
773-528-7464
Ages newborn to 3 years

Sing n' Dance is loved by parents and children alike on the northside of Chicago. Long before the boom in mommy and me classes, Sing n' Dance offered developmentally appropriate music and movement classes. Classes include playground time, circle time and an opportunity to meet other parents. A 10-week session is $150 for babies less than 10 months and $180 for babies 10 months and older. Street parking is available in the morning. Sing n' Dance offers free valet parking beginning late morning for the infant classes. (See Chapter 5 for information about their fantastic Parent & Toddler Nursery School.)

Suzuki Method

The Suzuki Method was developed by Shinichi Suzuki and is based on his belief that "musical ability is not an inborn talent but an ability that can be developed." The Suzuki Method involves not only the child and their teacher but also the parent. It believes that talent is developed in a nurturing environment, and parents, as an integral part of this, attend all classes with their child. Therefore, if the child is learning to play the violin the parent too will participate so that what is learned in class is supported and reinforced in the home. Usually, the child and parent take a weekly individual lesson and a weekly group lesson with other students at his or her level. Typically, lessons are $30 for a half hour and group lesson fees are determined separately depending on the length of the lesson. Below is a list of schools that teach the Suzuki method and the instruments offered.

Andersonville Suzuki
1502 Edgewater Avenue
773-271-4406
Ages 3 and older
Violin and viola
Street parking.

DePaul Community Music Program
804 West Belden, Room 328   www.music.depaul.edu
773-325-7262
Ages 5 and older
Piano, viola, violin, cello, flute and guitar
Parking passes are available for classes after 3:00 PM and cost $20 for a year or street parking.

Gold Coast Music School
1137 North State Street
312-587-0159
Ages 3 and older
Violin and cello
Street parking.

Sherwood Conservatory of Music
1312 South Michigan Avenue   www.sherwoodmusic.org
312-427-6267
Ages 3 and older, depending on the instrument
Cello (at age three), piano, violin, viola, flute, harp and guitar (at age four)
Street parking or there is a nearby paid parking lot.

Suzuki Music School of Lincoln Park
1753 North Fern Court
312-266-9587
Ages 4 and older
Violin, cello, piano and recorder
Street parking.

www.suzukimusiclp.com

Suzuki-Orff School for Young Musicians
1148 West Chicago
312-738-2646
Ages 4 and older
Violin, viola, cello, guitar, flute and piano
Street parking.

www.suzukiorff.org

Suzuki-Orff School for Young Musicians
1148 West Chicago
312-738-2646
Ages 6 months and up

www.suzukiorff.org

The Suzuki-Orff School for Young Musicians was founded in 1981. The school's unique approach to music education emphasizes the partnership among the student, parent and teacher. This approach is combined with the Orff method, which is based on the premise that children learn through a natural child rhythm. This method employs games, activities and movement as a springboard to musical experiences.

The school occupies a building in Chicago's West Town neighborhood with street parking. For children as young as six months it offers the Baby STEPS program, which uses rhymes and songs. Toddlers participate in the Learning Explorers One or Two class, in which children sing, play rhythm instruments and do movement games. Private and group lessons on the violin, viola, cello, guitar, flute and piano begin at age four (see Suzuki section). Seventeen-week sessions are offered. Prices vary depending on whether children are enrolled in a group class or private lesson. Scholarships are available.

(See Catchall section for additional music classes.)

Dance

Ballet d'Enfant
3234 North Southport
773-477-4488
Ages 2–9 years

This is the perfect place for a young ballerina to begin lessons. The environment is enchanting, especially for young girls mesmerized by pink tutus and princesses. Classes are constructed around a fairytale theme in which the teacher reads the story and the ballerinas act it out, complete with costumes. For children ages two to three, Ballet d'Enfant offers classes with a caregiver. Children ages five-and-a-half and older begin to learn the fundamentals of ballet technique. Summer and holiday camps are offered. Classes are $275 for a 16-week session. Street parking.

Belle Plaine Studio
2014 West Belle Plaine
773-935-1890
Ages 3–13 years

Belle Plaine Studio is a unique space that was once a horse stable. The studio is run by a mom who knows first-hand what makes for a fun dance program. The studio offers ballet, jazz, creative dance, tap, tumbling and yoga. Classes run 14 weeks for $125. The environment is casual and welcoming. Street parking.

Chicago Ballet Arts
7416 North Ridge Boulevard   www.chicagoballetarts.com
773-381-1000
Ages 2 and older

At Chicago Ballet Arts children ages two to four years begin their dance experience in creative movement classes, then move on to pre-ballet and ballet. A structured environment with live piano accompaniment, Chicago Ballet Arts, strives to create a love of dance at an early age. A 12-week session is $120. Free parking is available in their attached lot.

Hyde Park School of Ballet
5650 South Woodlawn   www.hydeparkschoolofballet.org
773-493-8498
Ages 3 and older

The Hyde Park School of Ballet offers ballet, jazz, flamenco, tap, modern dance and creative movement classes for children. The school has an extensive schedule to accommodate even the busiest toddler or preschooler. Each session ends with a recital. The school also offers trial classes to make sure that your would-be ballerina is committed to attending class. The creative movement classes are $120 and pre-ballet is $175 for 16 weeks. Street parking.

Krivoy
1145 West Webster Avenue
773-248-1466
Ages 4 years and older

Krivoy is an adorable studio in Lincoln Park that offers a dance and movement class that is highly popular with boys. The teacher introduces different cultures and allows for lots of play and improvisation as part of the class. Classes are $120 for the toddler class and $160 for the preschool class for an 8-week session. Street parking.

Ruth Page School of Dance
1016 North Dearborn Parkway   www.ruthpage.org
312-337-6543
Ages 3 years and older

The Ruth Page School of Dance is a serious dance arts center for your would-be dancer. Ballet (pre-ballet for younger ones), tap and jazz are taught weekdays and weekends. Classes are long. At age 5, my daughter took an hour and a half class. An added benefit of taking dance at Ruth Page is that the acclaimed teachers use some French in addressing the children. Classes are $66 for six weeks. Free parking in the small parking lot.

The School of Ballet Chicago
218 South Wabash, 3rd Floor   www.balletchicago.org
312-251-8838
Ages 3 years and older

The School of Ballet Chicago is a structured dance school that provides creative movement classes beginning at three years old. Located in the Loop, additional classes are offered in Lincoln Park at the Menomonee Center. One of the big thrills of taking ballet at this school is that even the youngest dancers get to participate in the annual Highlights of The Nutcraker production. The school offers fall, winter and spring terms ranging in price from $150 to $187.50 for a weekly class. The school validates parking tickets for the lot next to the school.

(See Catchall section for additional dance classes.)

Art

Gymboree Play & Music
3158 North Lincoln Avenue   www.gymboree.com
773-296-4550
Ages 18 months to 5 years

Gymboree offers GymARTS I and II for toddlers and preschoolers. Gymboree has teamed up with Crayola to create a program that allows kids to paint, sculpt and explore different textures and mediums. Classes also include singing, story time and movement activities. Classes are $279 for a 12-week session. Street parking.

Hyde Park Art Center
5307 South Hyde Park Boulevard   www.hydeparkart.org
773-324-5520
Ages 2 years and older

The Hyde Park Art Center is a 60-year-old fixture in the Hyde Park-Kenwood community. In addition to its exhibits, the art center runs education programs for the community. Children's programming begins at age two and expands significantly for children five and older. Children can explore art in a number of different mediums including painting, drawing, ceramics and more. The building has a great old, alternative art scene feel to it and the teachers are very engaging. Classes are $110 for members/$130 for nonmembers for a 10-week session. Street parking.

Lill Street Art Center
4401 North Ravenswood   www.lillstreet.com
773-477-6185
Ages 2 years and older

At Lill Street Art Center, children as young as two work with clay alongside their parent or caregiver. Some art classes include story time and songs. Older children can work in other mediums such as, charcoal, watercolors and acrylics. The new studio on Ravenswood is beautiful and includes a casual café that serves light snacks. Classes run for 10-week sessions and start at $140. A wonderful feature of Lill Street is that it provides great day camps whenever Chicago Public Schools have a day off—a real parent saver! Street parking.

Spark Your Art
1450 Webster Place   www.sparkyourart.com
773-330-1322
Ages 2 years to adult

Spark Your Art offers a variety of classes for young artists. Each week children can work in different mediums, such as paint, clay, collage work, etc. Classes are continuous and can be purchased in discounted packs of ten for $225 or individually for $25 each. Best yet, Spark Your Art will customize classes for a small group of children (two or more). Street parking.

Ukrainian Village Children's Center

918 North Damen

http://uvcc.home.mindspring.com

773-342-7415

Ages 2½–5 years

Artist, teacher and mom, Sarah Boone provides weekday art and play classes most days of the week. Her classes last for two hours and include arts-and-crafts, stories and play time. The center is full of imagination-stirring toys and activities, such as a sand table filled with dinosaurs, small tree logs and of course cups. There is a play kitchen, wooden blocks, Lincoln logs, trains and more. Art activities are process-oriented where kids experiment with clay, paint, fabric and more. The art center is stocked with jars of beads, seeds, rice, popcorn and more for kids to use in their projects. Classes are from 9:30 to 11:30 in the morning. Parents can participate or drop off the child. The classes are a bargain at just $10 each (siblings pay $8). On Saturday's, drop-in classes are offered and usually include older children. The Ukrainian Village Children's Center is a treasure! Street parking is easy.

(See Catchall section for additional art classes.)

Theater

Emerald City Theatre
Apollo Theater
2540 North Lincoln Avenue
773-529-2690
Ages 3–8 years

www.emeraldcitytheatre.com

Emerald City Theatre offers a new education program for young children. The first class, "Theater Fun & Games," is designed for three- to five-year-olds and allows kids to play theater games and act out stories. This class is offered on Saturday mornings. For older children, ages five to eight, the theatre company provides "Dramatic Beginnings: Storytelling," a class in which children explore storytelling by creating and telling their own stories then acting out them. This class is offered on Thursday afternoons or Saturday mornings. Both classes are 8-week sessions and cost $100. The classes conclude with a recital. Street parking.

Lookingglass Education
2936 North Southport, 3rd Floor
773-477-9257 ext 193
Ages 1 to teens

www.lookingglasstheatre.org

Lookingglass offers energetic and imaginative programs led by a very talented staff. Some classes combine tumbling and art in their pursuit of imaginative play. The staff is very adept at building stories and inventive play, with input from kids, to create captivating fantasies. A number of different classes are offered for a variety of age groups. Children three and older can attend classes without a parent/caregiver. Street parking is easy. Lookingglass also has terrific summer and spring break camps.

The Second City
1608 North Wells Street
Piper's Alley 4th floor
312-664-3959
Ages 4 to teens

www.secondcity.com

Second City, long known for terrifically funny shows and its education and training center for adults, now brings the fun to kids. Its 50-minute classes are engaging and energetic. Children stretch their imaginations through basic improv games. An 8-week session is $120-$130. Street parking or paid parking in the nearby garage.

(See Catchall section for additional theater classes.)

Foreign Language

Alliance Francaise
810 North Dearborn Street   www.afchicago.com
312-337-1070
Ages 1 year and older

Alliance Francaise offers several programs for young children to learn French and enjoy French culture. For toddlers Alliance Francaise offers "Moms, Pops and Tots" and independent classes for children four and older. The classes are conducted in French and allow children to gain exposure to the language through songs, crafts, movement and of course, snacks. Classes are offered in 10-week sessions for $165. Street parking.

Language Stars
1777 North Clybourn   www.languagestars.com
866-55-STARS
Ages 1 to 10 years

Language Stars has grown leaps and bounds in the years since my daughter took her first class. The teachers use what they call the *FunImmersion* method in which children hear only the language they are being taught from the moment class begins until it ends. Classes are constructed around stimulating themes, such as outer space and the circus. Parent & tot and kids-only programs are offered. Summer camps are also available. Prices vary depending on which session you sign up for but the parent & tot and kids-only programs cost $390 for a 14-week session. Parent & tot programs are one hour; kids-only programs are 75 minutes. Street parking.

A fantastic program that defies categorization. . . .

Tiny Tykes
Lincoln Park Zoo   www.lpzoo.org
2200 North Cannon Drive
312-742-2053
Ages 2–3 years

Some of the best classes my son and I ever participated in were at Lincoln Park Zoo. The classes offer various animal themes and include a story, meeting an animal and a craft. Classes are held on Tuesdays and Thursdays. Each class is $12 for members and $15 for nonmembers. Classes fill up quickly so do not delay! Parking for a fee is available in the Cannon Drive parking lot or you may get lucky and find street parking.

Chapter 8

The Sporting Life

~ Catchalls ~ Hockey ~ Horseback Riding ~ Ice Skating ~ Martial Arts
~ Soccer ~ Swimming ~ Tennis ~ Tumbling/Gymnastics

It's a sporting life for today's toddlers and preschoolers. Even babies are getting in on the action at places such as Gymboree where classes start at infancy. These days it's not unusual for three-year-olds to take tennis lessons in the morning and ice-skating lessons in the afternoon. Living in the city, it is vital to know about facilities where children can run around and work out their energy, as most of us do not have large backyards to gather in for rounds of hide and seek or neighborhood kickball games.

As in the previous chapter on classes I have included a category called "catchalls" to cover organizations that offer a breadth of sports programs.

Catchalls

Chicago Park District
www.chicagoparkdistrict.com
312-742-PLAY
Ages 18 months and older

The Chicago Park District offers a wide range of physical play and sports programs for young children. Programs offered include gymnastics, bitty basketball, t-ball, softball, baseball, ice-skating, peewee soccer, swimming, tiny tot tumbling, hockey and more. The programs offered vary at each park district so you must research which park districts offer the program you want. The Chicago Park District's Web site is a great way to do this. The Web site enables you to search for programs

based on park district name, zip code, keyword, program or age group. You also can pick up a program catalogue at any park district building just prior to registration. Registration for classes is four times a year in conjunction with the change of the seasons. Registration recently became easier now that the park district sets aside a certain portion of the spaces for registration online.

Hyde Park Jewish Community Center (JCC)
Start Smart Sports   www.goJCC.org
5200 South Hyde Park Boulevard
773-753-3080
Ages 3 to 5 years

The Hyde Park JCC offers "Start Smart Sports" a program created by the National Alliance for Youth Sports (NAYS) for children three to five years old. This program is designed to introduce young children to soccer, t-ball and basketball in a fun, noncompetitive manner. Toddlers and a parent (or caregiver) participate in the program together. In addition to the onsite instruction, children receive the necessary equipment to play at home, a jersey and a parent's manual. The Start Smart program is $99/members and $129/nonmembers for a 6-week session. The center also provides "Sport Shorts" during the winter/spring months, which give kids a chance to play a variety of sports.

The Hyde Park JCC also offers swimming, flag football, gymnastics, ice-skating and Tae Kwon Do. (The parent/tot swimming program and swim lessons occur at the nearby Regent's Park Club Pool.) Prices vary depending on the class. Call for a schedule. Free parking is available in the attached lot.

Lakeshore Athletic Club
1320 West Fullerton   www.lsac.com
773-477-9888
Ages infants to teens

Aside from meeting mom and dad's fitness needs, Lakeshore created numerous programs for children. Children can enjoy tennis, tumbling, martial arts, karate, various dance classes, swimming, yoga, basketball, soccer, football and t-ball. In addition to these athletic programs, Lakeshore offers music, art and foreign language classes—all under one roof. This family friendly club has a family recreational pool and sponsors Friday "Video Pizza Parties," and "Family Fit and Fun Nights" in which kids are able to participate in a number of different sports. Nonmembers may sign up for one class session but after that the family must become members to participate in the club's programs.

Lakeshore offers a "Pee Wee Club" for two- and three-year-olds from 9:00 AM to 12:00 PM Monday–Friday. In this program children have playtime, participate in arts, circle time and swimming. Lakeshore also sponsors summer camp beginning at age two. Members receive a significant price discount. A 10-week class is $95 for members and $165 for nonmembers. Free parking is available in the attached lot.

Lincoln Park Athletic Club

1019 West Diversey
773-529-2022
Ages 4 months and older

www.lpaconline.com

Lincoln Park Athletic Club (LPAC) offers a parent/tot swim program for its members for children ages four months to three years. Members and nonmembers can participate in swim classes, available to children ages three-and-a-half to six years. Lessons are $90 for an 8-week session for members and $120 for nonmembers. LPAC also offers member family swim hours on Saturday and Sunday evenings. In addition, LPAC provides a variety of children's programs for members including rock climbing, yoga, creative movement dance, ballet and karate. Parking (with validation) available in the attached parking lot.

Menomonee Club for Boys and Girls

224 West Willow Street
312-664-4631

www.menomoneeclub.org

Drucker Center
1535 North Dayton Street
Ages pre-kindergarten to 6th grade

Menomonee Club provides just about every sport your child might want to participate in. Sports programs offered include basketball for boys and girls, baseball, girls softball, t-ball, track and field, girls on the run, flag football, girls field hockey, soccer, kayaking, judo, tumbling, even fencing. The minimum age for participation in sports programs fluctuates depending on the program. Membership is $60/child/year and reduced rates for classes are available to members. The price of sports programs varies depending on the program. The Drucker Center has a parking lot. Street parking only for the Menomonee Clubhouse on Willow Street.

YMCA

Ages 6 months and older

www.ymcachgo.org

Chicago has many YMCA branches throughout the city and suburbs. The physical play and sports programs vary depending on each of the branches. Four YMCA's that offer a wide range of sports programs include the Lake View, Irving Park, New City and the South Side Y. For specific details call the Y you are interested in. But to give you an idea of the breadth of programs offered at the Ys I have listed below some of their information.

Irving Park YMCA

4251 West Irving Park Road
773-777-7500

Lakeview YMCA

3333 North Marshfield Avenue
773-248-3333

www.lakeviewymca.org

New City YMCA
1515 North Halsted
312-440-7272

South Side YMCA
6330 South Stony Island
773-947-0700

The YMCAs offer every sports program your child could want! Children can participate in tumbling, gymnastics, basketball, soccer, floor hockey and Tae Kwon Do. Members receive a significant price discount on programs. For example, the soccer program is $25 for Y members and $50 for nonmembers per session. Many of the Ys have an extensive swim program, including lessons and family swim times. Classes are offered almost every day of the week at every level for every age group. Children three years and younger must participate with a parent or caregiver. Older children can take lessons independently. Swim classes are $40 for members and $80 for nonmembers for an 8-week session.

A fantastic feature of the South Side Y is the children's pool. It is only two feet, nine inches deep throughout. The pool is in a separate enclosed room and provides toddlers a safer place to swim. The South Side Y also has a mini-golf course. It does not have the decorative features we have come to expect from putt-putt courses but it is a fun place for young kids to play. The Lake View Y offers exercise classes for mom and baby including "Walk-a-baby" and Social Stroll. Each of the Ys listed above has an attached parking lot.

Hockey

Johnny's IceHouse
1350 West Madison
312-226-5555
Ages 6 and older

www.johnnysicehouse.com

Once children have mastered Johnny's IceHouse's "Learn to Skate" program they can graduate to hockey lessons. In this class children learn basic hockey skills. All participants must wear full hockey equipment. A 9-week session is $161.

McFetridge Sports Center
3843 North California Avenue
312-742-7585
Ages 3 and older

www.chicagoparkdistrict.com

Young, would-be hockey players can get their start at the McFetridge Sports Center. Children start in the Penguin Clinic where they learn the fundamentals of skating for hockey. The class is $50 for eight weeks. The center has a concession stand at which light snacks are sold. Free parking is available in the attached lot.

Horseback Riding

Hannaberry Farm
27712 South Klemm Road
Crete
708-946-9935
Ages 3 and older

www.hannaberry.com

When your 38-pound child wants to take horseback riding lessons you need to find an instructor you can really trust! My daughter Abby began horseback riding lessons at Hannaberry Farm when she was five and absolutely loves it. Denise Hanna is a remarkable instructor (and a professional storyteller), who teaches children not only on how to ride but how to care for and respect a horse. Lessons are conducted in outdoor or indoor arenas, depending on the weather. Private lessons are available for children three and older; group lessons are available for children ages 7 to 15. A private, half-hour lesson is $30; an hour is $50. Group lessons are $25/hour. Lessons can be bought at a discount if purchased in packages of five or 10. Crete is about an hour and fifteen-minute drive from the city.

Palatine Stables
Palatine Park District
1510 North Northwest Highway
Paletine
847-359-0009
Ages 1 and older

www.palatineparkdistrict.com

Palatine Stables is an excellent place for young children to begin horseback riding. It has multiple outdoor arenas and two indoor arenas so lessons continue year round. Beginning at age one your child can go for a pony rides. Short rides are just $5 and a half-hour ride for the more enthusiastic rider is $12. Older kids who take riding lessons at the stable lead pony rides. Pony rides are available on the weekends and on Monday and Wednesday afternoons. The park district also offers private lessons for children five years and older. A half-hour private lesson is $39. Group lessons begin at age eight. Palatine is about a 45-minute drive from the city. There is a small store at Palatine Stables that sells helmets, boots, riding pants and more.

Ice Skating

Johnny's IceHouse
1350 West Madison
312-226-5555
Ages 2 and older

www.johnnysicehouse.com

At Johnny's IceHouse tots as young as two take to the ice (with mom or dad) for ice skating lessons. Beginning at age four, kids take lessons independently. Johnny's IceHouse, is a great facility, that teaches kids how to skate by using a "walker" to support them. First-time skaters get lots of attention because of the low student to teacher ratio—it is five students to one teacher. All kids must wear helmets and bring their own skates, as Johnny's IceHouse does not rent skates. The only food available is from vending machines. Lessons are $196 for a 12-week session. Street parking.

McFetridge Sports Center

3843 North California Avenue www.chicagoparkdistrict.com
312-742-7585
Ages 3 and older

McFetridge Sports Center has a great indoor ice skating program. The center has a concession stand at which light snacks are sold. Lessons are $42 for eight weeks and $32 for six weeks. Very affordable! Free parking is available in the attached lot.

Many other Chicago Park Districts offer outside ice skating lessons during the winter months. Visit the Web site for details.

(See Catchall section for more information.)

Martial Arts

ATA Taekwondo

3103 North Ashland Boulevard
773-755-4065
Ages 3 and older

Children as young as three begin martial arts training at ATA Taekwondo. Through this program children gain new physical abilities and a strong sense of self because instructors place an emphasis on self-discipline, self-respect and respect for others, such as mom! Instructor, "Ms. Kim, " a teacher since 1996, has a great way with kids. She recognizes that children learn differently and changes her teaching to work with each child. Children are welcomed to attend for up to a month for free before committing to ensure that they like the class.

H.M.D. Academy of Tae Kwon Do

1442 West Belmont www.taekwondochicago.com
773-549-0285
Ages 4 and older

Children and parents can take Tae Kwon Do lessons together at the H.M.D. Academy. Tae Kwon Do helps children gain discipline and build their self-esteem. Children can take lessons with a parent or independently. The Academy has experience working with children with special needs, such as autism, Attention Deficit Disorder/Attention Deficit Hyperactivity Disorder and physical limitations. Lessons also are taught at the Nettlehorst Elementary School and open to the public. Two free introductory classes are available. Class fees vary; call for details.

(See the Catchall section for additional martial arts classes.)

Soccer

The American Youth Soccer Organization (AYSO)
800-872-2976   www.soccer.org
Ages 4-1/2 and older

There are several regional AYSO chapters in Chicago. If you are interested in your child playing on an AYSO team go to its Web site where you can enter your zip code to find the team closest to you. AYSO is incredibly popular so you must register on the day registration opens.

(See Catchall section for additional soccer programs.)

Swimming Lessons

East Lakeview Multiplex
Located in the New York condo building   www.multiplexclubs.com
3657 North Pine Grove
773-477-3664
Ages 6 months and older

The East Lakeview Multiplex provides group and individual children's swim lessons. Lessons are available to families even if they are not members of the club. One lesson is $40 (for nonmembers), a 6-lesson package is $37.50 each, and a 12-lesson package is $35 each. Swim lessons for children whose families are members are offered at a reduced rate. Group lessons are also available. The East Lakeview Multiplex is located in the New York condo building. Parking is available in the building. The Multiplex validates parking tickets so guests pay a reduced fee of $2.

Latin School "Learn to Swim" Program
59 West North Boulevard   www.latinschool.org
312-582-6515
Ages 4–12 years

During the winter months of November–February the Latin School runs the "Learn to Swim" program on Saturdays. There are three different levels from beginners to intermediate. The 11-week session is $155. Street parking.

North Pier Athletic Club
474 North Lake Shore Drive   www.fitnesswave.com
312-464-3300
Ages 6 months and older

The North Pier Athletic Club offers swim lessons for members and nonmembers. Beginning at six months children take swim lessons with a parent. Children three and older take group lessons, divided by ability, or private lessons. A session (three classes) is $40 or three sessions (nine classes) are $90. Free parking (with validation) in the building garage.

(See Catchall section for additional swim programs.)

Tennis

McFetridge Sports Center
3843 North California Avenue   www.chicagoparkdistrict.com
312-742-7585
Ages 3 and older

McFedtridge Sports Center is a great place for your toddler or preschooler to try her/his hand at tennis. Lessons for tots are offered year-round in this indoor sports center. You cannot beat the price; lessons are $28 for eight weeks. The center has a concession stand that sells light snacks. Free parking is available in the attached lot.

Mid-Town Tennis Club
2020 West Fullerton Avenue   www.midtowntennisclub.com
773-235-2300
Ages 4 and older

Mid-Town Tennis Club brings its professional approach to tennis to your toddler. The club is membership based but children's lessons are available to nonmember families too. Beginning at age four, preschoolers are taught the basic elements of tennis in a fun and positive environment. Mid-Town can provide the racquets. Classes are $202 for a 13-week session. Free parking is available in the attached lot.

Tumbling/Gymnastics

Gymboree Play & Music
3158 North Lincoln Avenue   www.gymboree.com
773-296-4550
Ages newborn–four years

Gymboree offers play programs for children from birth to four years. The play space is beautifully designed with fun and challenging setups that change weekly and encourage kids to climb, crawl and explore. Classes are offered in 12- and 24-week sessions. A 12-week session is $195 and a 24-week session is $359. A one-time enrollment fee of $25 is required. Children enrolled in a Gymboree class can participate in open gym play three times a week. Street parking.

Lakeshore Academy
937 West Chestnut   www.lakeshoreacademy.com
312-563-9400
Ages 6 months and older

Lakeshore Academy offers a variety of movement, tumbling and gymnastic classes for babies and older children. For the older and serious gymnast, Lakeshore Academy trains award winning competitive teams. Another great urban treasure is the "Hidden Peak" climbing wall where kids as young as five learn to rock climb in small classes. The Academy also offers Karate lessons. The staff is incredible and Lakeshore has a terrific reputation among parents. A 5-week session cost $90 for members and $115 for nonmembers. Lakeshore offers summer and winter camps. Free parking is available in the attached lot.

The Little Gym
3216 North Lincoln   www.tlgchicagoil.com
773-525-5750
Ages 4 months to 12 years

The Little Gym allows toddlers and bigger kids to tumble, swing and gain their balance on real gym equipment. The gym offers parent/child classes for babies and young children. Kids three and older participate solo. The staff is enthusiastic and knowledgeable and the facility is large and colorful. The gym has a bright waiting area where parents and siblings can watch the activity. Also available are fun, creative and flexible summer camp programs for toddlers and older children. Classes cost $150 for a 10-week session. There is an additional $40 annual family membership fee. Street parking.

Peterson Park District
5801 North Pulaski
312-742-0490
Ages 18 months and up

www.chicagoparkdistrict.com

Peterson Park is part of the Chicago Park District but it requires a special mention in the gymnastics category because it offers such an outstanding program for toddlers through young adults. In fact, their competitive gymnastics team, beginning for children six years and older, is award winning. Peterson Park provides more than 20 weekly "Mom's Dad's, Tot's Gymnastics" classes for toddlers 18 months and older. For children ages three to five years Peterson Park offers more than 40 weekly "Twinkle Star Gymnastics" classes. It is a beautiful facility and there is an attached parking lot. And because it is the park district you cannot beat the price. Classes start at $40 for a 10-week session.

Skyline Gymnastics
4430 North Western Avenue
773-478-7174
Ages 18 months and up

Skyline Gymnastics offers a competitive and challenging program for young gymnasts. The program director and head coach of the competitive team, Dianne Durham, was a member of the U.S. National Team and was the United States All Around Champion.

Toddlers participate in parent/tot classes, preschoolers attend independently, and beginner gymnastic programs start for children seven and older. The gymnasium is large with plenty of space for parents and siblings to sit and watch the action. Classes are $125 to $185 (depending on the length of the class) for an 8-week session. Street parking.

(See Catchall section for additional tumbling & gymnastic classes.)

Chapter 9

The Great Outdoors in the Big City

~ Playgrounds ~ Sledding ~ Ice Skating ~ Beaches
~ Pools ~ Big Outdoor Adventures

One of the fabulous things about raising children in Chicago is that you never need to venture far to find a great playground. I cannot begin to list all the wonderful playgrounds in our city. If you ask most parents what their favorite park is they are likely to name their neighborhood playground or park. This is because Chicago has such terrific parks with everything your child could want. However, when you want to explore beyond your neighborhood park here are some great ones worth the extra effort. Some of the parks listed are attached to a field house, which means they have bathrooms and I was able to include a phone number. All of these parks have easy street parking.

Playgrounds

Adams Park
1919 North Seminary
312-742-7787

Adams Park is very fun, with great shade, lots of different play equipment, a sandbox and a separate large water park. This park is attached to a park district building and offers bathrooms—yippee!

Bixler Playlot
57th and Kenwood

This recently renovated park is a hot-tot-spot in Hyde Park. There are soft mats under the playground equipment, a spray pool and grassy areas for playing chase or throwing a ball.

Cummings Playground
Lincoln Park West & Dickens
(Across from Lincoln Park Zoo)

We always combine a visit to this park with a trip to the zoo. It's a fun park with a large play structure and a smaller one for toddlers. My kids love it because it contains animal sculptures that kids can climb on and act out their jungle fantasies.

Fellger Playlot
Belmont & Damen

Even though this newly renovated park is located at a busy intersection it has a kiddie-urban-oasis feel to it. The park has play equipment for both small tots and older children. There is a small water play area in the summer and open spaces for kicking a ball around or having a snack. There are no bathrooms.

Harold Washington Park
Between 51st and 53rd Street, just East of Hyde Park Boulevard

This is a remarkable park with two large play structures, swings, a sandbox, a pirate ship and a spray pool. The park also has a pond for sailing model boats. It's a fun park for young children until late afternoon when school gets out, at which time older kids play and hang out in the park, which makes it difficult for smaller tykes to compete.

Horner Park
Montrose to Irving Park & California

Horner Park is a huge park next to a park district building so there are bathrooms and a parking lot. There is a nice play lot with equipment for kids of different ages. The park offers great winding bike paths, perfect for kids to ride tricycles or big kid bikes. It also has a lot of open space to fly a kite or throw a ball.

Humboldt Park
1440 North Sacramento Avenue
312-742-7549

Humboldt Park is a huge park with multiple play structures, a fishing lagoon, a spray pool, lots of open space and a beautiful field house. This is a fun park to let your child loose on his or her tricycle or bike. There is plenty of parking and of course bathrooms in the field house.

Indian Boundary
2500 West Lunt Avenue
312-742-7887

Indian Boundary is an extraordinary park made almost completely out of wood. It has great equipment to crawl through and climb on, which allows children to weave all through this massive structure. With that said, there are some challenges. It is difficult to get a "visual" on your child as he/she climbs his/her way through all the different levels. Secondly, because of the play structure's size, it's hard to manage two kids at different ages, abilities or interests. I like to go with a friend who has children my kids' ages, so we can tag-team. One of the coolest features of this park is the small zoo that contains a handful of animals. There are also large open spaces great for picnics, ball games and kites! Bathrooms are located in a nearby park district building.

Juniper Park
Greenview/Waveland

Juniper Park was recently redone and has a soft surface to ease falls. This park also has a big sand box. On beautiful days the park is packed! An added bonus is that this park has a water sprinkler system during the summer. So bring a change of clothes!

Kenwood Community Park
Kenwood and 49th Streets

Kenwood Community Park is a terrific neighborhood park. It is a large park with a lot of open space that includes baseball fields. The park has equipment for toddlers and older children. There is a small park district field house with bathrooms!

Millennium Park
Michigan/Randolph

Millennium Park is Mayor Daley's crown jewel. It highlights the best of Chicago; our phenomenal and free cultural events, our spectacular skyline and our commitment to open spaces, all of which make Chicago such a "livable" big city. World-renowned architect Frank Gehry created the Pritzker Music Pavilion. As with much of Chicago's remarkable architecture, people love it or hate it. I think it's spectacular! The new Music and Dance Theatre is also located in the park. The park also features gardens, lots of open space to run, the McCormick Tribune Ice Rink, and a small cafe and restaurant.

A favorite kid's destination is "The Cloud Gate Sculpture" by artist Anish Kapoor, nicknamed "the bean". It is an intriguing sculpture for kids and adults alike. Children love walking under it and viewing their numerous reflections. My kids' favorite part of the park is the unique water fountain. It features two towering LCD screens with the faces of Chicagoans on it. Water streams down from them and occasionally the faces "pucker" to spout water from their mouths onto willing recipients. The fountain area is full of children splashing and squealing in delight! The park has large nice bathrooms. Parking is easy in the Grant Street Garage. Millenium Park has quickly become a favorite and frequent downtown destination for families!

Morrie Mages Playground
Irving Park at the lake

Morrie Mages is a fun and large park. Located by the lake, it stays cooler for longer in the spring. The park has a large layout, which is a challenge if you bring more than one child. There are bathrooms, but they are located a short hike away at the field house.

Oz Park
2021 North Burling Street
312-742-7898

Oz is a great park complete with replicas of the Wizard of Oz characters to mark each entrance to the park. Oz offers a large open play area and a sweet garden that kids can walk through for a quieter time. The park has large, wooden playground sets and as mentioned in the description of Indian Boundary Park, it is hard to track or retrieve kids. This park is very shady, which makes it a great summertime spot. The only bathroom facility offered is a port-a-potty.

Ravenswood Manor Park
Eastwood/Manor/Francisco

This is a wonderful park tucked away in a gorgeous neighborhood. It was recently updated and has terrific play equipment for kids of all ages. It is quiet except for the street level brown line train that runs by the park—close enough to thrill train-obsessed toddlers. The park also has a small, open spaces for ball play or picnics. There are no bathrooms.

Sunshine Playground
Cannon Drive, just south of Diversey

Sunshine Playground is a fun, tucked-away park by North Pond. The playground has two large wooden structures, one for young toddlers and another for bigger kids. Bring some bread to feed the ducks!

Supera Playlot
Lill & Racine

Supera Playlot is a cute park and very manageable with multiple kids. There is a sand box and a great boat structure for your young pirate.

Wells Park
Montrose, bordered by Lincoln & Western

This huge open space encourages kids to run! The park has a good-sized play lot, although it's older equipment. A beautiful gazebo was recently added to the park, which makes for a fun picnic spot or shady place on hot days. Bathrooms are nearby in the park district building.

Wicker Park
1425 North Damen Avenue
312-742-7553

This is a wonderful park, currently undergoing a major renovation. Wicker Park is an epicenter for parents raising their families in Wicker Park and Bucktown. The park is large with open space to play, a baseball field, a park district building (which means bathrooms), a pretty water fountain and separate play structures for toddlers and bigger kids. As part of the renovation, the park will have water play sculptures. Wicker Park hosts a farmer's market during the summer months. The park has bathrooms.

Wrightwood Park
2534 North Greenview
312-742-7816

Wrightwood Park is a large, open park with separate play equipment for older and younger children. The park also has a soft turf to ease falls. A good feature of this park is that it is next to a park district building and therefore offers bathrooms! This park also has an adorable pool (see section on pools for details).

Sledding

Sledding with toddlers is an ambitious endeavor that usually involves more exercise for mom and dad than the kids! Once your toddler is bundled up, she or he is probably as wide as she or he is tall, making walking, especially up a sledding hill, a challenge! That said, sledding with your kids is a winter highlight. Below, I have listed our two favorite Chicago sledding hills.

Cricket Hill
North of Montrose Avenue at Lake Shore Drive

When Chicago turns into a winter wonderland, bundle up your tots for some fun sledding on the hill just west of Montrose Harbor. Parking is easy and free. The hill is quite manageable for even the youngest tots but still a thrill for older children. Unfortunately, there are no nearby bathrooms. So when your child announces he or she has to go to the bathroom and you find yourself unwrapping layer after layer so that he or she can go behind a tree in the cold and snow—just consider it part of the adventure!

Sledding Hill at Soldier Field
312-235-7000   www.soldierfield.net

Complete with a snowmaking machine this snow hill is the place to go when it's cold outside but there is no snow on the ground. The parking situation is a bit confusing as the closer lots

(McCormick Place) were closed (when we visited) and the new museum campus parking lot is a bit of a hike with tots in tow. Most people park illegally on the street right by the sledding hill—when there is no traffic. If you are going to sled here and plan on parking in the garage, prepare to pull your child on the sled all the way (or carry her/him if there is no snow on the ground). It's too far for a child to walk in cold weather. There are no bathrooms nearby.

Ice Skating

There are numerous outdoor skating rinks operated by the Chicago Park District between late November and the end of February (or later depending on the weather). For a complete list visit the Chicago Park Districts' Web site, www.chicagoparkdistrict.com or call 312-742-PLAY.

Daley Bicentennial Park
337 East Randolph St.　　　　　　　　　　　www.chicagoparkdistrict.com
312-742-7648

This is a great place to ice skate. You have all the beauty of downtown without the crowds of the newer McCormick Tribune Ice Rink. It is $2 to rent skates and there is a $2 adult and $1 child rink fee. This rink is very easy to navigate with kids. You can park in the Monroe Street Garage and enter the facility from the Randolph Street side of the parking garage. Bathrooms and lockers are available in the park district office.

McCormick Tribune Ice Rink
Millennium Park　　　　　　　　　　　　　　www.chicagoparkdistrict.com
55 North Michigan Avenue
312-742-5222

The McCormick Tribune Ice Rink is such a fun and easy place to ice skate with kids. Simply park in the Grant Park North Garage and take the elevator directly into the building where you rent skates. Rink time is free and skate rental is $5. The rink is open from late November through mid-March. The ice rink also has a nearby restaurant, the Park Grill (312-521-PARK). The Park Grill features kids' favorites, such as grilled cheese, burgers, chicken fingers and mac & cheese. Bathrooms are available in the building.

Midway Plaisance Park
1130 North Midway Plaisance　　　　　　　　www.chicagoparkdistrict.com
312-745-2470

Midway Plaisance Park is a great place to ice skate because it is rarely crowded. Ice skate rentals are $3 a person. It is free to ice skate except after 3:00 PM and on the weekends when it is $4 for children and $5 for adults. It has an indoor facility with bathrooms.

Beaches

Chicago Park District manages the beaches along 24 miles of Chicago's lakefront. The beaches are open Memorial Day through Labor Day from 9:00 AM to 9:30 PM. For information on beach hours and fees call the Chicago Park District's designated phone line at 312-742-5121. Some beaches have better amenities for families than others. My favorite beaches with kids are listed below.

Foster Beach, 5200 North

Foster Beach is a great beach for families. This beach offers free parking, public bathrooms and a concession stand. The best feature of this beach is the renovated outdoor showers and spigots for cleaning up sand—and popsicle-covered kids! It has a specially designed mat that creates a level, smooth path over the sand for handicap accessibility. This path also makes it easy to push strollers or pull wagons onto the beach. This beach has bathroom facilities.

Loyola Beach, 7000 North

Loyola Beach is a very accessible beach. You can park close to the action in metered parking spaces. There is a large playground if kids grow tired of the beach. Heartland Café operates a small eatery next to the playground. This beach has bathroom facilities.

Montrose Beach, 4400 North

Montrose Beach is nice because it is not as crowded as the other beaches. Parking is fairly easy and free. There are few amenities, but if you want a beach where kids can run free, this is it. One challenge is that because it's not a popular beach it has a smaller staff of lifeguards. If you set up "camp" where there is no lifeguard on duty, then a lifeguard (from further down the beach) will ask you to move to the portion of the beach she or he is stationed at. This beach does not have water spigots to rinse off sandy children. There is a small concession stand and bathrooms between the Montrose and Wilson entrances.

North Beach, 1600 North

North Beach is very family friendly. It has nice bathrooms and a number of eating facilities including a roof-deck, sit-down restaurant. This beach also has the specially designed mat for handicap accessibility. This means easy stroller/wagon access too. The small parking lot at North Beach fills up quickly and it is not free. Fee parking is also available at the zoo parking lot on Cannon Drive. After parking in this lot, you can use the pedestrian overpass to cross Lake Shore Drive. This beach also rents bikes.

Oak Street Beach, 1000 North

This beach is great for people watching! It also has the handicapped accessible mat described above, a restaurant and equipment rentals, such as bikes and roller blades. The bathrooms are not in the best of shape. There is a great beachside restaurant and it has port-a-potties for customers. There is no parking nearby. This beach is accessible from the Michigan Avenue underpass.

57th Street Beach, 5700 South

57th Street Beach is accessible from the Promontory Point underpass or 56th Street. My friends who live near this beach report that it is at times a difficult beach to enjoy due to frequent beach closings. Beaches are closed when there are high bacteria counts in the water. My friends report there also is a big problem with broken glass. So remember water shoes for children. The beach has bathrooms, showers and a snack bar.

63rd Street Beach House, 6300 South

The 63rd Street Beach House is a stunning structure complete with a Promenade Deck. There is a concession stand and restrooms. Like the 57th Street Beach, this beach experiences frequent closings due to high bacteria counts.

About our beaches...

Each year Chicago residents experience many beach closings due to high bacterial counts in the lake. It is always a bit unnerving to discover that the beach your family played at yesterday is closed today due to high bacterial counts in the water. I do not have a grasp on why we have such frequent beach closings, however, in my quest for more information my family has joined the Lake Michigan Federation.

Lake Michigan Federation is a non-for-profit organization committed to conserving our beaches, eliminating toxins in the lake and restoring fish and wildlife. It is a very family-friendly organization that hosts beach clean-up days. Whole families can participate! With memberships starting at just $25 a year, it's a worthy investment in our lakefront. One of the changes many of us experience upon becoming a parent is a greater concern and commitment to the environment. Joining the Lake Michigan Federation is a small step each of us can make to ensure that we enjoy our beaches not only as parents but also as grandparents. Visit their Web site at www.lakemichigan.org.

Pools

The pools listed below are all outdoor pools run by the Chicago Park District or the Cook County Forest Preserve. They are a select few that I consider to be among the best. Many were recently remodeled. Park district and forest preserve pools have lots of rules. For example, some forbid strollers and bags from the pool deck. This is for safety reasons. I have never understood how a parent can be expected to bring a baby or toddler to a pool and not have a big bag full of necessities within hands reach at all times. Call ahead to find out if the pool you plan to visit allows bags on the pool deck. Other challenging rules include no floats and frequent swim breaks. It can be hard to get a firm grasp on all the rules and the times that the pool is open to the public. However, these are nice facilities and most are free!

Portage Water Playground and Pool
4100 North Long Avenue
312-742-7634

This park district has a large pool for swimming and a smaller zero-depth pool with a water play structure. The water gets fairly deep around the water park structure and young toddlers can find it difficult to keep their balance. Pool hours are a bit fickle because they are often closed for camp use. Get a schedule and keep it handy. Also, you are not allowed to bring bags or strollers into the gated water park area. Street parking is easy.

River Water Playground and Pool
5100 North Francisco
312-742-7516

This is a deep pool that can be great fun for children with some swimming skills. Because the water is about four feet at its shallowest I find it a difficult pool for toddlers who like to get in and out of the water on their own. No bags or strollers are allowed on the pool deck. A good feature of this pool is the newly built water park. The water park is enclosed separately from the pool so young children can play freely and safely. Street parking is easy.

Wrightwood Park
2554 Wrightwood Avenue
312-742-7816

I love this pool. It's very small and only three feet deep throughout. It is the perfect pool for the child gaining independent swimming skills. It can get a bit crowded. Sometimes you have to wait to get in, but they rotate all swimmers every 45 minutes, so the wait is never too long. It also has a small, "scary" bathroom (in the words of my seven-year-old) so plan on wearing your bathing suit so you won't have to change there.

Wheylan Pool Aquatic Center
6200 West Devon Avenue
773-775-1666

www.fpdcc.com

This large and beautiful pool draws a crowd. Come early to avoid long lines. The pool features a small baby/toddler pool and a large, zero-depth pool complete with a water park in the middle. My family and I have had a lot of fun at this pool. There is a large parking lot and a concession stand. This pool is operated by the Cook County Forest Preserve and is not free. Admission is $5 per person, $3 for children ages 4–12; under three years the children are free.

Private pools

In my quest for the perfect pool experience I have found a couple of private pools associated with large condo/apartment buildings. For a fee, families can obtain a season membership. These include Sandburg Terrace and Regents Park Club. These pools are especially good options for families with older children because the pools are usually around three feet at their shallowest. Also, these pools do not offer all the bells and whistles of water playgrounds that suit babies and toddlers.

Regents Park Club
5050 South Lake Shore Drive
773-288-5050

Regents Park has an indoor pool with a retractable roof so it is fun all year long. The club offers valet parking. Currently there are no children's swim lessons. Family memberships (two adults, two children) are available for $127 for one month, $911 for six months and $1318 for 12 months.

Sandburg Terrace
1355 North Sandburg Terrace
312-787-5700

Summer memberships are available for the Sandburg Terrace pools. The memberships go on sale in mid-April and are discounted through the end of May. Memberships can be purchased for $588 for a family of four at Fitplex, located at 1235 North LaSalle. Sandburg Terrace has two pools (the South pool, close to Division Street, and the North pool, close to North Avenue) and you can go to either one. The pools do not have concession stands (though you can bring your own food) and there is street parking only.

Big Outdoor Adventures

Children's Garden at Soldier Field
Museum Campus Drive   www.soldierfield.net

The Children's Garden is a great addition to Chicago's fabulous museum campus. While not really a destination in itself, it is a very fun stop on your way to one of the museums. The garden was created in a "bowl" so it is not visible from the sidewalk or street. As you walk up to the garden you discover a play area enclosed by grassy hills. The garden has earth themes with atypical activities including a fantastic climbing sphere, a tunnel to crawl through and low-lying sculptures for kids to crawl on. All are designed to inspire children's creativity about the earth and galaxy. Parking is available at the museum campus garage for $12. There are no bathrooms nearby.

Diversey Miniature Golf Course
Diversey Parkway & Cannon Drive
312-742-7929

This mini golf course is a hidden treasure along Chicago's Lincoln Park. Tucked behind the tennis courts this mini golf course is rarely crowded. It is a great place for even the youngest put-putters to give it a whirl. The course has 18 holes and is $5.50 for kids and $6.50 adults. A great bargain. Parking is affordable at $1 for an hour and $3 for two hours. There are bathrooms.

North Park Village Nature Center
5801 North Pulaski   www.cityofchicago.org/environment
312-744-5472

The North Park Village Nature Center is a 46-acre nature preserve and educational facility in the northwest part of the city. The nature center includes more than two miles of trails around wetlands and forest. Adventurers can choose from shorter or lengthier trails, depending on the age and stamina of your tykes. An educational facility provides animal and plant artifacts, such as deer antlers and tortoise shells that children can handle. There is also a secluded room where families can read books, play with animal puppets and draw. Lastly, the center has a classroom where nature classes are taught for toddlers, preschoolers and older children. Do not miss the periodic "campfire songs and stories" where families gather in the woods at night to listen to nature stories, sing songs and enjoy roasting marshmallows. The center offers an abundance of programming so get on their mailing list. There is a large, free parking lot and bathrooms with changing tables.

Osaka Garden on Wooded Island
Jackson Park
5900 South Lake Shore Drive
312-747-6187

Just south of the Museum of Science and Industry is a beautiful, secret garden, called Osaka Garden. The winding path and large stepping-stones that my son can follow across the pond enchant him. The garden, a gift from Japan for the 1893 World's Columbian Exposition was recently renovated. It has a Japanese Tea House that my son thinks is a stage and likes to perform on. The only non-child friendly aspect is the bridge you cross from the parking lot to Wooded Island. It does not have adequate horizontal bars and a child could easily slip through when checking out the view. There are no bathrooms nearby.

South Shore Nature Sanctuary
South Shore Cultural Center
7059 South Shore Drive
312-747-2536

www.chicagoparkdistrict.com

Once the South Shore Country Club, the South Shore Cultural Center is a striking building and the grounds are equally spectacular. The center is now part of the Chicago Park District. It is located on the shores of Lake Michigan and boasts a beautiful beachfront with lifeguards, a concession stand and bathrooms. But the best part of the grounds is the South Shore Nature Sanctuary. The Nature Sanctuary has sand dunes, a small wetlands area and a butterfly meadow. The nature walk takes about 20 minutes to complete. There is free parking and bathrooms outdoors (by the concession stand) and indoors in the park district building.

Chapter 10

A Year of City Celebrations
A Month-by-Month Guide

One of the reasons you likely chose to raise a family in Chicago is because of all the entertainment and fun events our city offers. There is so much to do, every week and weekend in Chicago. Usually, my family and I find ourselves choosing between fun opportunities, though we do have some annual can't-miss events! In this chapter I categorize the events month by month. As a Chicagoan, you can probably predict that the calendar is a bit light on events between January and April. However, for the rest of the year you will be in the enviable position of selecting one fun event over another.

With each of the events I provide the inside scoop as to how these events feel as a family and as a tired overworked parent. I also give you an idea of when to prepare yourself for a huge crowd and how best to steel yourself against it. As always, I include the bathroom report, parking information and snack options when appropriate. Enjoy!

January

Chinese New Year
Late January–mid-February, determined by the lunar calendar
Wentworth Avenue between Cermak and 24th Streets

The Chinese New Year parade occurs annually in Chinatown. The exact date is determined by the lunar calendar. This celebration includes fireworks, drums, gongs, cymbals and a gigantic paper dragon.

It is a very cold time of year to stand outside so bundle up! Manageable crowds and a reasonable parade length make this enjoyable with small kids. There are no port-a-potties. Your best bet is a restaurant or the public library. Parking is easy in a nearby parking lots.

February

Winterfest

A Sunday afternoon in late January or early February   www.chicagoparkdistrict.com
Daley Bicentennial Plaza
337 East Randolph

Chicago's Winterfest is a fun winter outing with a small-town feel. It includes ice skating, horse-drawn carriage rides, hotdogs, hot chocolate and more. Admittance is $5 a person. Daley Bicentennial Plaza is easy to access. Park in the Monroe Street Garage and take the stairs directly into the park district building where you pay for the event. There are bathrooms in the building.

Chocolate Fest

Weekend in early February   www.garfield-conservatory.org
Garfield Park Conservatory
300 North Central Park Avenue
312-746-5100

Yum! Come celebrate the only fruiting chocolate trees in Chicago. This fun, family event has children's activities and free samplings of different chocolates. Parking is easy in the attached lot. The bathrooms are equipped with changing tables.

Cupid's Corner Valentine's Day Dance

Friday or Saturday closest to Valentine's Day   www.chicagoparkdistrict.com
Held at numerous Chicago Park District locations throughout the city.

Take your youngest sweetheart out for an early night of dancing and celebration. Many park districts sponsor Valentine's Day Dances. Some specify Daddy/Daughter or Mother/Son. These are fun events that usually include crafts, snacks and, of course, dancing! Valentine's celebrations cost no more than $5 per family or are free. The bathroom and parking scenes vary at each park district.

March

Maple Syrup Festival
Mid-March, Saturday and Sunday   www.cityofchicago.org/environment
North Park Nature Center
5801 North Pulaski Road
312-744-5472

Just when you think you cannot find one more redeeming factor of our long winters, the North Park Nature Center comes to the rescue with this family event. Take this opportunity to show your child where the maple syrup he or she loves comes from *before* you buy it at the grocery store. Children experience the entire maple syrup making process from tapping the tree, to collecting the sap, to boiling it down into syrup to, finally, tasting it. There are also storytelling and crafts. Parking is easy and free in the attached parking lot. The Nature Center has bathrooms equipped with changing tables.

St. Patrick's Day Parade
Saturday before March 17th
Dearborn Street between Wacker and Van Buren Streets
312-744-3370

St. Patrick's Day is a can't-miss event in Chicago—even if you try. Not only is Chicago home to one of the largest parades in the country, the city goes the extra distance by dyeing the Chicago River emerald green—an impressive sight. Although this is a cold time of year to enjoy a parade, the school bands, bagpipes and impressive Irish step dancers are enough to captivate any young child. There are no port-a-potties. Parking is easy in the Grant Street Garage.

March or April

Easter Egg Hunt
Saturday morning prior to Easter   www.chicagoparkdistrict.com
Lincoln Park Cultural Center & other park district locations
2045 North Lincoln Park West
312-742-7726

The Chicago Park District lays out the red carpet for the Easter Bunny. At the Lincoln Park Cultural Center Peter Cottontail hides eggs for the kids and poses for pictures. There are also crafts, face painting, refreshments and more. Several park districts also offer "Breakfast" or "Lunch with the Bunny." Visit the park district's Web site to find locations. The bathroom and parking scenes vary at each park district.

May

Mayor Daley's Kids & Kites Festival
Weekend in early May & October   www.cityofchicago.org
Museum of Science and Industry

Go fly a kite! For free! This festival is a fun event for families and occurs in early May and October (at Montrose Harbor in October). Free kite kits are provided or families can bring their own. Instructors and kite-flying pros will share their talents. After your child has made and flown a kite it is equally fun to watch the experts show off their unique kites and kite-flying skills. There is also storytelling. There are port-a-potties. Parking is easy and free at Montrose Harbor. Parking is $12 at the Museum of Science and Industry.

Bike the Drive
A Sunday in late May from 5:30 AM to 10:30 AM   www.bikethedrive.com
Lake Shore Drive, starts at Columbus & Balbo   www.cityofchicago.org
312-744-3315

Our mayor loves bikes! Once a year the city shuts down Lake Shore Drive from 5:00 AM to 10:30 AM and bikers take over the drive. Yes, the event is early! But I know you are up, so hit the drive for a unique experience. At this event you will see many bikers sporting a kid trailer and young kids on bikes. Children as young as four can participate in this event if they are experienced riding among other bikers. Younger children can enjoy the event by riding in a trailer. The event includes a 15- or 30-mile ride. Bikers must start the ride at Columbus and Balbo and can only get off at designated spots. If you and your youngster are not up for a 15 mile ride you can turn around at a designated spot. My daughter and I turned around at Fullerton—far short of the 15 miles. This is not a spontaneous event. To decide if you and your children are up for it visit the Web site to learn more. Participants must pre register. It is $35 for adults, $20 for children and includes a free t-shirt. There are port-a-potties.

June

Taste of Chicago
End of June–First week in July   www.cityofchicago.org
Grant Park

It is estimated that 3.6 million people attend the Taste of Chicago—think about that! The Taste is a ten-day annual Chicago event that includes food, entertainment and activities. Many families enjoy the Taste. Bring a stroller or wagon because this event is crowded and difficult to keep up with wiggley toddlers. Weekdays are definitely more manageable than weekends. The earlier you arrive the better. To make it easier on families, the Taste provides a Parent/Helper tent with free diapers and changing tables! Admittance is free and food is available for purchase with tickets. In 2004, eleven tickets were $7. Dominick's sells tickets (a week prior to the Taste) at a discount of 11 tickets for $5.50. Port-a-potties are available and there are numerous nearby public parking lots.

Winnetka Children's Fair

Sponsored by the Winnetka Community Nursery School
Usually the second Friday & Saturday in June
Village Greeen
Winnetka
847-446-4432

The Winnetka Children's Fair is the only suburban event I included in a year of celebrations but it is a can't-miss event. For more than 50 years the Winnetka Community Nursery School has organized this fair as a school fundraiser. The fair includes carnival rides, crafts, games, tasty treats and a children's theater show. The crowds get heavy in the afternoon so we always arrive at 10:00 AM when it opens. The primary lunch item is hotdogs so pack a sandwich if your child does not like them. Each ticket is $1 and most rides require 2–3 tickets. Tickets are sold in advance for a 5 percent discount. Street parking is easy. There are port-a-potties.

July

Independence Eve Fireworks Spectacular

July 3   www.cityofchicago.org
Navy Pier

Chicago's annual Fourth of July fireworks display is difficult to manage with kids. Prime viewing spots are claimed early in the day. Imagine Navy Pier covered with people that you have to walk through and push a stroller around. You get the idea. Park anywhere you can (Navy Pier will fill up early). There are bathrooms everywhere at Navy Pier.

Chicago Folk and Roots Festival

The second weekend in July   www.oldtownschool.org
Wells Park
Lincoln/Montrose
773-728-6000

The Chicago Folk and Roots Festival is great fun for the entire family. This two-day event attracts musicians from around the world. Performances run simultaneously on several stages. There is a kid's music tent that features fabulous music and dance entertainment. Food is available from vendors. A quiet children's play area allows families some down time. The event costs $5 for adults, $1 for children. A complete schedule is available online. There is a small public parking lot on Lincoln, just north of Wells or neighborhood street parking. There are plenty of port-a-potties.

La Fiesta del Sol

Thursday–Sunday, in late July   www.fiestadelsol.org
Cermak Road, between Throop & Morgan

Experience the largest Mexican cultural event in the Midwest. Although large (1.5 million attendees over a four-day period), it maintains a nice family feel. Kids will enjoy carnival rides, a petting zoo, traditional Mexican dancing, pony rides, crafts, local musicians and of course Mexican cuisine. Port-a-potties are available.

The Children's Festival
Summer on Southport
A Saturday & Sunday in mid-July; 10:00 AM– 4:00 PM   www.southportneighbors.com
3800 block of Southport

Just what kids need—a festival exclusively for them. The Southport Children's Festival is a fun, annual event that features musical entertainers, tasty treats, games, crafts and kid-oriented vendors. In past years the event included fantastic children's musicians such as Ralph's World, Justin Roberts and Nelson Gill, and the Caribbean Rhythm Band. This event also offers carnival games, arts & crafts, a pet parade and food. Port-a-potties are plenty and street parking around the neighborhood is available.

Annual Venetian Night
Late July/early August   www.cityofchicago.org/specialevents
Montrose Harbor between the Chicago Yacht Club and Shedd Aquarium

Many Chicagoans regard Venetian Night as one of the best summer events of the year. The accompanying fireworks are the most sensational of the summer. This event is a bit late for kids, but worth it. It features more than 35 local boats decorated with lights, which promenade along the lakefront while the Grant Park Orchestra performs. The event culminates with fantastic fireworks at 9:30 PM at Monroe Harbor. Parking is easy at Grant Street Garage or Monroe Street Garage.

August

Air & Water Show
Mid-August   www.cityofchicago.org/specialevents
North Avenue Beach & Oak Street Beach

Get your battle plan ready—it is worth the effort. Chicago's Air & Water Show is a spectacular event that brings more than two million people to the lakefront for this two-day event. The show features U.S. Air Force Thunderbirds, the U.S. Army Parachute Team, The Red Baron Stearman Squadron, the Lima Lima Flight Team, the Aeroshell Aerobatic Team and the Shell Extreme Watershow. While this event is awe-inspiring to watch, it is a bit tricky to attend with young children. There are several ways to go about it. Take public transportation and bring a stroller, a blanket, snacks and more. I also have known families to park a car (completely loaded with strollers, wagons, coolers and more) close to the lakefront very early in the morning before the crowds arrive. When it's time to head to the event they take public transportation or a cab to their parked car (strategically pre-packed) and head over to the lakefront. Whatever works! There are port-a-potties.

September

57th Street Children's Book Fair
A Sunday afternoon in late September

A family favorite! The 57th Street Children's Book Fair is one of my favorite annual events. It's a fun and pleasant time that features storytellers, crafts, children's musicians and, of course, great books for sale. The event is not too crowded. Book vendors are small, independent sellers that include Powell, Magic Treehouse and, of course, 57th Street Books. There are no food vendors, but several restaurants along 57th Street that you can pop into, including a Hyde Park institution—the Medici Bakery. There are no port-a-potties. Nearby street parking is available.

October

Autumn Festivals at Park Districts

Hamlin Park, 3035 North Hoyne   www.chicagoparkdistrict.com

Horner Park, 2741 West Montrose

Oriole Park, 5430 North Olcott

Oz Park, 2021 North Burling

Peterson Park, 5801 North Pulaski

Portage Park, 4100 North Long

Warren Park, 6601 North Western

A number of Chicago Park Districts transform themselves into "country pumpkin patches" for a Saturday in October each year. These events are held on separate Saturdays throughout the month so even the busiest family can go to one. My family and I have gone to Horner and Oz Parks multiple times. They all include a mixture of the activities such as pumpkin painting, hayrides, pony rides, face painting, games and petting zoos. These events are very popular so go early to beat the crowds. Admission is free. Individual activities charge a small fee. There is some food available and port-a-potties. Parking and bathroom options vary at each park district.

Chicago International Children's Film Festival
Late October   www.cicff.org
Various locations
773-281-9075

The largest children's film festival in the country is in our backyard! The Chicago International Children's Film Festival features more than 200 films, videos and animated shorts for ages three (at the youngest!) to 13, care of Facets Multimedia. Movies are shown during the week and through the weekend. Most of the movies are foreign films and therefore in languages other than English with English subtitles. By reading the movie descriptions you can get a good idea of which films will be most appropriate. Parking and bathrooms vary at each location.

Chicagoween

Mid-October through 31st
Mayor's Office of Special Events
312-744-3370

www.cityofchicago.org/specialevents

Chicago loves Halloween. Every year this holiday seems to grow bigger. By the time the 31st finally rolls around I can barely work up the enthusiasm to go trick-or-treating, because we have participated in so many activities all month.

Listed below are some of the highlights of "Chicagoween."

Pumpkin Plaza

Daley Plaza
Daily throughout the month of October

For most of October, Daley Plaza is transformed into "Pumpkin Plaza." This engaging event includes daily performances by the Midnight Circus. Kids also can decorate pumpkins, wander around the haunted village and listen to ghost stories. This fun event is for young toddlers and older children. There is no designated parking lot and no bathrooms on the plaza.

Boo Ha Ha

Saturday afternoon in late October
Lincoln Park Cultural Center
2045 North Lincoln Park West
312-742-7726

www.chicagoparkdistrict.com

The Lincoln Park Cultural Center hosts a thrill-filled event, "Boo Ha Ha," suitable for very young children. Kids wear their costumes to this fun event where they play games, do crafts and select a pumpkin from the pumpkin patch. There is street parking or a paid parking lot south of the Cultural Center. There are bathrooms with changing tables in the center.

Navy Fear & Fun

Throughout the month of October
Navy Pier
312-595-JACK

www.navypier.com

Still looking for more Halloween activities? Check out Navy Pier's "Navy Fear & Fun," during the entire month of October. My older child still has not ventured into the Kids Haunted House. There are great decorations that cover the entire pier—and fun, free crafts for younger children. Also trick-or-treating occurs every Thursday night from 5:00 to 9:00 PM throughout the month of October and, of course, on Halloween. Parking is expensive at Navy Pier; there are plenty of bathrooms equipped with changing tables.

Spooky Zoo Spectacular

Last Saturday of the month before Halloween, noon to 2:00 PM   www.lpzoo.org
Lincoln Park Zoo
2200 North Cannon Drive
312-742-2000

Kids wear their costumes to this annual event at the zoo. The zoo is decorated in fun but not scary Halloween decorations. Costumed characters wander about the zoo while kids trick-or-treat. It does get very crowded so go early. This is a good Halloween event, especially for very young children because it is not scary. Parking is available on the street or in the zoo lot on Cannon Drive for $12. Each building has bathrooms equipped with changing tables.

More Chicagoween events . . .

Finally, the Field Museum, the Shedd Aquarium, the Museum of Science & Industry, the Adler Planetarium, the Peggy Notebaert Museum and the Chicago Cultural Center all host special Halloween events in late October. Call each museum for specific details.

November

The Magnificent Mile Lights Festival

The Saturday prior to Thanksgiving
Michigan Avenue (from Oak Street to Wacker Drive)

Kick off the holiday season with The Magnificent Mile Lights Festival. This event is fun but crowded. Throughout the day Disney characters perform live holiday musical shows outdoors at Pioneer Court. At 6:00 PM Sorcerer Mickey Mouse leads a procession of floats and magically lights more than a million lights from Oak Street to Wacker Drive. In the past I found myself lifting two children above the crowds but the alternative of staking out a spot earlier means missing the shows at Pioneer Court and being really cold for a long time. The event culminates in a spectacular holiday fireworks show over the Chicago River, but visible all along Michigan Avenue. You can park in any garage off of Michigan Avenue. There are no port-a-potties.

Chicago's Thanksgiving Parade

Thanksgiving Day, 8:30 AM   www.cityofchicago.org
State Street from Congress to Randolph

Macy's Thanksgiving Parade has got nothing on Chicago! Our parade is fun and accessible, albeit much smaller. The parade is not too crowded—my children were able to make their way to the front and we sat on the curb with them, in front of the standing crowds. Holding toddlers on one's shoulders gets old pretty fast. The parade features high school marching bands, horseback riders, and large floats, as well as clown performances by Ringling Brothers and Barnum & Bailey Circus, plus gargantuan balloons including a Rescue Hero, Strawberry Shortcake and more. It's an easy and fun way to kick off the holiday season. Park at the Grant Street Garage (on Michigan Avenue) and from there it's just a couple blocks walk to State Street. There are no port-a-potties.

Holiday Windows at Marshall Fields and Carson Pirie Scott
Thanksgiving weekend–the New Year
111 North State Street
1 South State Street

Every year, Chicagoans enjoy checking out Marshall Fields' holiday windows to see the current year's theme. In the past, favorite children's stories such as *Charlie & the Chocolate Factory*, The *Grinch Who Stole Christmas* and Paddington Bear were featured. Carson's holiday windows are equally magical. Parking is available in the garage just north of Fields or anywhere along Wacker Drive.

Annual Tree and Menorah Lighting
Friday after Thanksgiving   www.cityofchicago.org
Clark and Washington

The day after Thanksgiving you and your family can welcome the holiday season when you attend the annual City of Chicago Holiday Tree and Menorah Lighting Ceremony at Daley Plaza. The event begins at 4:30 PM. This annual ceremony is a child's first opportunity to chat with Santa. Park in any Loop garage. No port-a-potties.

Daley Plaza Santa's House
Friday after Thanksgiving–December 24   www.cityofchicago.org
Clark and Washington

Each year after Thanksgiving Santa Claus arrives to the Daley Plaza to hear kids' wish lists. Santa is available from 11:00 AM to 8:00 PM everyday (except from 3:00 to 4:00 PM when he is busy feeding his reindeer). The event is free and photos are available for purchase. Park in any Loop garage. No port-a-potties.

Christmas Around the World
Thanksgiving week–early January   www.msichicago.org
Museum of Science and Industry
773-684-1414

Every holiday season the main floor of the Museum of Science and Industry is filled with Christmas trees. The museum's annual *Christmas Around the World and Holiday of Light* gives visitors a glimpse of how countries around the world celebrate Christmas. If possible, avoid the opening weekend of Thanksgiving—it is a zoo! Parking is available in the museum's garage for $12. The bathrooms are large and equipped with changing tables.

Zoo Lights Festival

Lincoln Park Zoo

www.lpzoo.org

Saturday, after Thanksgiving–Sunday after January 1st;
Thursday–Sunday nights, 5:00–9:00 PM
2200 North Cannon Drive
312-742-2000

The Zoo Lights Festival is so much fun for the whole family. Each winter the zoo is transformed into a magical, holiday paradise! More than a million lights in the shapes of animals and holiday symbols make this event a must-see. There are ice sculptures, a giant maze, indoor crafts and the carousel. Over the years we have been on wonderfully, freaky warm December nights, during magical snowfalls and on bitter cold nights when my children could hardly move they were so bundled up. Whatever the weather, this is a "can't miss" annual event. The event is free! Parking is available in the zoo lot along Cannon Drive for $12. There are bathrooms equipped with changing tables in all the buildings.

John Hancock Center and Observatory

Thanksgiving week–New Year's

www.hancockobservatory.com

875 North Michigan Avenue
888-875-VIEW (8439)

During the holiday season there is so much to do and see on Michigan Avenue. Don't forget to visit the trains at the John Hancock Center. *The Hancock Holiday Mountain Railroad* is a 1,400-square-foot model train exhibit—featuring 11 trains circling around several holiday towns and rural scenes, including the North Pole, a ski slope, a farm, a carousel and much more.

Also, venture up to the 94th floor for spectacular views of Chicago and beyond. Then visit with Santa and Mrs. Claus. Admission is $9.75 for adults and $6 for children older than four and includes a free photo with Santa. If you intend to visit with Santa, plan on going on a weekend as Santa is only at the Hancock on weekends. Paid parking is available in the building and is accessible from Chestnut and Delaware Streets.

December

(Many of the events listed in November are holiday events so they continue into December)

Waldorf School Winter Festival

First Saturday in December, 9:00 AM–4:00 PM

www.chicagowaldorf.org

1300 West Loyola Avenue
773-465-2662

A true winter highlight! My family loves it. There is something for everyone at this event. Young children (my son's been going since he was 20 months) delight in the "Children's House," where they purchase a sack of golden nuts (25 cents each) then shop with the assistance of older children from the school. Handmade items are available for purchase and include miniature boats, dolls, jewelry, candles and more. Another favorite activity is candle dipping. Children (and adults) walk in a circle around many buckets of hot wax dipping wicks into them again and again, until a candle is formed. In the background live music is playing. There are numerous craft activities. For example, children decorate candles and small votive candleholders, and make holiday ornaments and more. These make great family and friend gifts.

Also, there is terrific holiday shopping. Unique handmade items like wooden animals, play tree houses and magical costumes for pirates, princesses and knights are sold by local vendors. This is a can't-miss event! No need to go home for lunch. The school sells pizza, sandwiches, hummus, fruit and many, many homemade sweets. There are plenty of bathrooms throughout the school. Street parking.

Dance Along Nutcracker

Sunday in early December   www.cityofchicago.org
Chicago Cultural Center
78 East Washington Street
312-744-6630

The Dance Along Nutcracker is a unique event in which professional dancers perform portions of the Nutcracker, then invite children in the audience to join them. This event is very popular. Arrive early to get a good seat. The event is free and there are no assigned seats. Parking is available in any nearby Loop garage. Bathrooms are equipped with changing tables.

Lucia Celebration

Saturday evening in mid-December   www.samac.org
Swedish American Museum
5211 North Clark Street
773-728-8111

A girl from the Scandinavian community, wearing a crown of lighted candles and flowing robes, leads the Lucia Celebration. Starting at the Swedish Museum, the girl, holding candles, leads the community up and down Clark Street. Everyone sings the famous Santa Lucia hymn. All the shopkeepers along Clark Street stand at their doors with lighted candles. It is quite a sight to see and experience. The parade ends at the Swedish Museum, where everyone is welcomed in the main hall for drinks, Swedish cookies and to sing more carols. Bathrooms are available inside the museum. Street parking.

Winter Solstice

Closest Saturday to the Winter Solstice   www.cityofchicago.org
North Park Nature Center
5801 North Pulaski Road
312/744-5472

North Park Nature Center's celebration of the Winter Solstice is a surprisingly popular event given that it is mostly outdoors, at night and the week before Christmas! It's a great way to celebrate yet another milestone of the December holiday season. Wooded paths are lined with candlelit lanterns that enable visitors to take a quiet, winter evening stroll in the woods (my kids, being city kids, never want to walk too far into the woods). Children can make outdoor, edible ornaments for the birds and squirrels on their block. There is an outdoor shadow show that is backlit by a huge bonfire. If you would rather be indoors, there is live music and warm cider to enjoy. There are bathrooms inside the Nature Center. There is plenty of free parking in the attached lot.

Kwanzaa: The Exhibition
DuSable Museum of African-American History   www.dusablemuseum.org
740 East 56th Place
773-947-0600

DuSable Museum offers a festival to celebrate the Kwanzaa season with food, fun and entertainment. The event is $10 for adults, $5 for children and a reduced rate for museum members. Reservations are required. There is a small, free, museum parking lot or street parking. Bathrooms are large and equipped with changing tables.

Mayor Daley's 4th Annual Holiday Sports Festival
The weekend and Monday post-Christmas,   www.cityofchicago.org/specialevents
call for exact dates each year
McCormick Place
2301 South Martin Luther King Drive
Mayor's Office of Special Events, 312-744-3315

Maybe I'm a wimp, but the words "McCormick Place" and "family outing" create some anxiety. It's no easy feat to take the family to McCormick Place, but there are times when it is worth it. The Holiday Sports Festival is one of those times. It is the perfect antidote for a family who has spent days cooped inside with too many relatives and plastic toys. So, if you are game the first thing you will need is a stroller, or better yet a wagon. The parking lot is a long distance from the building and the building is humongous. Don't make my mistake of thinking a three-year-old can walk that distance or you will find yourself carrying everyone's coats, the diaper bag and giving children rotating piggyback rides.

The Sports Festival features a "tot zone." This includes a large whale kids climb through, gymnastic equipment, short basketball hoops, bowling, golf and big wheels. There is a fishing pond in which kids practice casting, a large jumping jack, a super slide and much more. Bathrooms are convenient, clean and plentiful. A café (cafeteria) is conveniently located in the middle of the activity. There is also a McDonalds and Connie's Pizza one floor down. Admission is free and parking is discounted to the rate of $7.

The LaSalle Bank Winter Wonderfest at Navy Pier
Mid-December– first weekend in January www.navypier.com
Navy Pier
700 East Grand Avenue
312-595-PIER

Wow! You won't believe all the thrilling activities offered for children of all ages at this annual event. 2002 was the first Winter Wonderfest and my family hit it four times. Your family's enjoyment of this event depends upon how early you get there as the lines are ridiculously long as the day grows later. Ideally, tag team this event with another adult. That way one adult can wait in line for the next activity while the kids are enjoying an activity under the watchful eyes of another adult. There is something for every kid at Wonderfest. Fun attractions include an indoor ice skating rink, giant slides, rock climbing, a merry-go-round, a train ride, model trains, giant inflatable jumping toys, roller skating, bungee jumping, cookie decorating and much more. There are long lines at the bathroom so plan accordingly. Light snacks are sold within the fest and include popcorn, hot dogs, nachos, candy, juice boxes and beer. For a more substantial lunch you have to trek the distance toward the center or front of the pier, where most of the restaurants are located. This event costs $12 per person. Coupons for half off (for up to four people) are available at LaSalle Bank ATMs, which are conveniently located throughout Navy Pier. Parking is expensive at Navy Pier's garage.

Rockin' New Year's Eve
December 31st 2:00 PM and 4:00 PM seatings www.chicagoparkdistrict.com
Lincoln Park Cultural Center
2045 North Lincoln Park West
312-742-7726

The Lincoln Park Cultural Center is known for great events throughout the year and New Year's Eve is no exception. The party is perfect for young revelers. It starts at 2:00 PM (a second seating is at 4:00 PM) and includes pizza, party hats, noisemakers, live music and a countdown (although a bit preliminary) to the New Year! Kids toast the New Year with M&M filled plastic champagne glasses. Tickets are $5 and must be purchased in advance. This event sells out! Call in early December. Street parking only.

New Year's Eve Celebration
Lincoln Park Zoo www.lpzoo.org
2200 North Cannon Drive
312-742-2000

If ringing in the New Year with your family once it is actually dark outside has more appeal then try the *ZooLight's New Year's Countdown*. This event begins at 8:30 PM and counts down to a "Happy Zoo Year" at 9:00 PM. It is free! Parking is available in the zoo lot along Cannon Drive for $12. There are bathrooms equipped with changing tables in all the buildings.

Chapter 11
Suburban Excursions

Fun Places to Play and Explore Outside the City

Arlington Race Track

2200 West Euclid
Arlington Heights
847-255-4300

www.arlingtonpark.com

It's off to the races! The Arlington Race Track is a surprisingly fun family destination. Older kids (around five) enjoy placing bets on horses for 50 cents to a dollar. Make sure when you bet on a horse you bet for it to "place" or "show" as that increases the fun and your chances of winning! Each race lasts only two to three minutes and a new race begins every 30 minutes to give you a chance to place a bet. There are primarily bleacher seats. There are some tables, but get there early to stake out a spot. The food is typical sports arena eats—hotdogs, pizza, etc. Once a race ends it is fun to go down to the "winner's circle" where kids watch the horse receive its medal. However, much to my daughter's disappointment they don't let you pet them! Races are generally May through September, (Wednesdays through Sundays). You can valet park for $10. The bathrooms are large and equipped with changing tables.

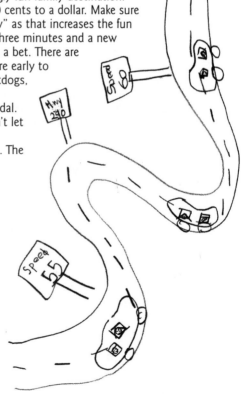

Bronzeville Children's Museum

www.bronzevillechildrensmuseum.com
Evergreen Plaza
96th Street and Western Avenue
Evergreen Park
708-636-9504

The only African-American children's museum in the country is in our backyard. The Bronzeville Children's Museum, just five years old, is off to an impressive start. Mother-and-daughter team—Peggy Montes and Pia Montes—launched the museum. Pia Montes leads children through the small museum at the beginning of each hour. She follows a set format with a brief educational presentation, an arts-and-craft activity, a short film and playtime. The museum's theme changes annually in February in honor of Black History month. Due to the museum's structured format it is best suited for kids four and older. Because the museum only changes its exhibit annually, it is not a place where you will go frequently, however, do not miss the opportunity to visit from time to time. It's an eye-opening and fun experience for children to discover the many unknown achievements of African Americans. Also, just visiting opens up a dialogue between you and your child about our country's past treatment of African Americans. The museum costs $3 for adults and $2 for children. It is open Tuesday–Saturday from 10:00 AM to 4:00 PM. It is located in a mall with a food court (McDonalds, pizza, Chinese food and more). There is no bathroom in the museum but one is nearby in the mall. Parking is free in the mall parking lot.

Brookfield Zoo
3300 Golf Road   www.brookfieldzoo.org
Brookfield
708-485-0263

Like the Lincoln Park Zoo the Brookfield Zoo is open every day of the year with extended summer hours. The zoo has wonderful exhibits, a number of which are large indoor facilities, making it a good destination year round. My kids' favorite aspect of the zoo is *The Hamlin Family Play Zoo*. There, kids pretend to be veterinarians, zookeepers and gardeners. The veterinary clinic is especially impressive. As pretend veterinarians, kids attend to various stuffed animals on authentic tables, use stethoscopes and other medical tools. An outdoor play area is made of recycled items. There is a separate fee for visiting *The Hamlin Family Zoo*. The zoo is an expensive destination. Entrance to the zoo is $8 for adults, $4 for children three and older. *The Hamlin Family Zoo* charges an additional fee $3 for adults and $2 for children. Admittance to the *Hamlin Family Zoo* is free Tuesdays and Thursdays, October–March. It costs an additional $8 to park. There are numerous places to eat throughout the zoo, though some places are open only during warmer months. Bathrooms can be found in each building exhibit or restaurant.

Bunny Hutch Novelty Golf & Games
3650 West Devon Avenue
Lincolnwood
847-679-9434

The Bunny Hutch is Chicago area's best miniature golf. Its two 18-hole courses are full of ramps, curves and tunnels sure to challenge older kids. The youngest golfers enjoy Humpty Dumpty, mermaids, dinosaurs and tree houses. There is a snack bar. The Bunny Hutch is open from April 1st through mid-October. The prices vary and depend on the time of the day you visit. Before noon it is $5 a person. From 12:00 PM–6:00 PM it is $6 a person. In the evenings it is $7 a person, except on Friday and Saturday nights when it is $7.50 a person. Parking is easy in the attached lot. Bathrooms are available.

Centennial Family Aquatic Center
2300 Old Glenview Road
Wilmette
847-256-9680

www.wilmettepark.org

While a bit of a drive from Chicago, my family and I find Centennial Family Aquatic Center one of our best swimming options. There is a terrific zero-depth pool for babies/toddlers complete with a small slide and water play area. Centennial also has a huge zero-depth pool with a water playground in the middle of it and two large, twisting drop slides. Finally, the last pool is deeper and a portion of it is sectioned-off for adult lap swimming. Floats and strollers are permitted. Admittance is $12 per person for nonresidents. Admittance to the toddler pool only is $8. Purchase a season pass if you plan to go often. For a family of three a summer pass is $230, for a family of four it is $254. The changing rooms are neat and the pool has several family changing rooms, complete with showers—very convenient! The bathrooms are typical pool bathrooms—very wet and a little messy. The concession stand serves pizza, candy ice cream and more. We usually pack snacks due to the long food lines. Parking is free.

Chicago Botanic Garden
1000 Lake-Cook Road
Glencoe
847-835-5440

www.chicago-botanic.org

The Chicago Botanic Garden is a fun outdoor adventure for the family. Young children are enchanted with the winding paths, water fountains, narrow bridges, rolling hills and wide-open spaces. Children can pick up the seasonal "eye spy," which will focus their visit as they search for pinecones, berries, etc. During the summer months the Botanic Garden adds the Jr. Railroad. It is a mesmerizing exhibit that features miniature trains, which move through plants, water, pebbles and other natural materials. This year *Thomas the Train* will join the Jr. Railroad. The exhibit costs $3 for children and adults and runs between June and October. There is a restaurant that serves grilled cheese, hamburgers, pizza, both indoors and outdoors. Older children enjoy riding their bikes along the bike trail. Strollers are allowed in the gardens, except for the Jr. Railroad. Entrance to the Chicago Botanic Garden is $8.75 per car. Bathrooms are large and equipped with changing tables.

DuPage Children's Museum
301 North Washington Street
Naperville
630-637-8000

www.dupagechildrensmuseum.org

The DuPage Children's Museum is such a treat and well worth the drive! It has many unique exhibits, all especially suited for very young children. The museum offers hands-on, manipulative play. Two of the fantastic exhibits include light rods where kids insert florescent rods into small holes to make patterns and a "3-D Me Pinscreen," which consists of thousands of straw-like tubes that children (and parents!) push in with hands or other body parts to create a 3-D image. The "Construction House" is amazing! In it kids use real saws, nails, hammers and other tools to shape their own piece of wood. The museum also has a great water play area, a wind tunnel and an art room.

Babies love the "young explorer" areas, which are designated for non-walkers. The "young explorer" sections are conveniently located throughout the museum so babies have safe, fun and developmentally appropriate places to play while older siblings enjoy the adjacent fabulous exhibits. I could go on and on but you should check it out for yourself. Bring your own lunch as the snack area has vending machines with limited choices. Make a bigger adventure out of it and take the Metra train, which stops in front of the museum. Parking is free in the large lot. Bathrooms are equipped with changing tables.

Emily Oaks Nature Center
4650 Brummel
847-677-7001
Skokie

The Emily Oaks Nature Center is a very manageable yet enthralling adventure for toddlers and older children. Young toddlers will enjoy taking a "hike" around the pond and spying chipmunks, bunnies, turtles, frogs and birds. The Nature Center has a terrific playground and a small indoor area where children can "track" various animals, complete with the animal's unique poop markings—FUN! The Nature Center also offers specific programs and family nights complete with campfires. The bathrooms are equipped with changing tables. No food is sold at the nature center. Parking is free. The nature center is a great find and FREE.

Enchanted Castle
1103 South Main Street
Lombard
630-953-7860

I can live happily without a return trip to Enchanted Castle although I do not think my son shares my feelings. Located in a strip mall, the Enchanted Castle is Chicago-area's largest indoor family entertainment center. It boasts a mini-golf course, lazar tag, a movie theater, a giant play-climbing station, bumper cars, a mini roller coaster and a large restaurant, the Dragon's Den, which serves beer for moms and dads! Many of the activities (the theater, lazar tag, the violent video games) are suited for school-age kids but my preschooler manages to find plenty to do. The Enchanted Castle also has *Kid's Quest,* a separate play space for younger children. This area has slides, balls, nets, pyramid towers and rope climbing. When kids enter *Kid's Quest* they are given a secure bracelet so they cannot leave the area without the parent being notified. Parking is free in the attached parking lot. Bathrooms are equipped with changing tables.

Exploritorium

4701 Oakton Street

Skokie

847-674-1500 ext. 2700

www.skokieparkdistrict.org

Another fun toddler-friendly place! The Exploritorium is housed in one large open room so it is an ideal place to take more than one child. There is great indoor play equipment, which includes a large climbing area with nets, tubes, tunnels and slides. A terrific water play area, dress-up clothes complete with a stage and a nice arts-and-crafts space are part of the fun. It costs $2 for children two and younger, $5 for older children and $2 for adults. It is open Monday, Wednesday and Friday from 9:00 AM to 6:00 PM and closed on Tuesday and Thursday. It is also open on Saturday from 10:00 to 3:00 PM. Bathrooms are equipped with changing tables. Parking is free in the large lot.

Fullersburg Woods Forest Preserve

3609 Spring Road

Oak Brook

630-850-8110

www.dupageforest.com

Fullersburg Woods is a fun outdoor adventure for toddlers and preschoolers. Nestled along Salt Creek, the woods was once strictly recreational but due to pollution problems was closed in the early 1970s. Soon after, efforts began to restore the habitat. Today Fullersburg Woods is committed to providing both recreation and environmental education. My son and I enjoy short walks along the five miles of trails. Particularly toddler-friendly is the quarter mile trail across a bridge and around an "island." The trail features frequent markers that encourage kids to engage all their senses, with ideas of what to look for, listen to, smell and touch. When you get to the "taste" sense, Fullersburg Woods uses this as an opportunity to educate kids about not eating berries. However, kids do get a chance to taste something. At the conclusion of the trail there is a water pump where parents help kids pump well water and have a drink. As you can imagine we spend most of our visit pumping water!

There are picnic tables but bring your own food because no food is sold. The bathrooms have that campy feel—kind of buggy and a little dirty. There is a small log cabin visitor center with hands-on activities, which include telescopes, binoculars, stuffed animals and a pretend bird's nest kids can climb into. Entrance and parking are free.

The Grove

1421 Milwaukee Avenue

Glenview

847-299-6096

The Grove is a treasure. You can lose yourself among the secluded trails and beautiful surroundings. The short trails are very manageable and fun for young tykes. There are narrow, more remote trails you can find if you follow a winding wooden walkway that turns into a narrow dirt path. My son was certain we were deep in the woods by this point. He dropped acorns and called me Gretel to his Hansel. There is much to enjoy year-round at the *Interpretive*

Center. The center offers a close look at live turtles, snakes, fish, and preserved bugs and creatures. Admittance is free and the parking is easy. The Grove is open seven days a week. Bathrooms are located in the *Interpretive Center.*

Health World

1301 South Grove Avenue   www.healthworldmuseum.org
Barrington
847-842-9100

Health World is a museum dedicated to the promotion of healthy bodies and lifestyles. It is full of interactive exhibits that get kids to think about and have fun with safety and healthy living. It is best suited for kids two and older. There are many fun areas to explore, which include an eye-popping, gargantuan-sized girl whose body can be explored from her "ouchies" to her heart and brain. There is a "Dark Crawl" exhibit that simulates the experience of being blind. In it kids must rely on other senses to get through a maze. Other health exhibits include a physician and dentist office and an emergency room, in which kids play physician or patient. A large safety exhibit allows kids to act out many scenarios, such as how to cross streets safely, watch for oncoming trains and escape a house in case of fire.

The museum has a nice cafeteria called "Georgi's Garden." It serves the usual kid favorites of chicken nuggets, grilled cheese, pizza and hamburgers. It also offers parent-friendly options such as soups and salads. The bathrooms are great with toddler-sized toilets, low sinks and even bathroom stalls large enough for a stroller! Admission is $6 for children two and older and $6 for adults. Parking is free and plentiful.

Heller Nature Center

2821 Ridge Road   www.hellernaturecenter.org
Highland Park
847-433-6901

The Heller Nature Center consists of many trails that young tykes like to explore. Strollers are allowed on the trails but bikes are not. The real attraction is the great lineup of family programs. In the winter children and parents can participate in Winter Fest, take a moonlit stroll in search of owls or help harvest maple syrup. In the summer the center hosts overnight family camping trips, canoe outings and nights around the campfire. The center has a bathroom but no food services. Admittance and parking are free.

Illinois Railway Museum

800-BIG-RAIL or 815-923-4000   www.irm.org
Union

Whether your child is *Thomas The Train* obsessed or not, she or he will enjoy a visit to the Illinois Railway Museum. The museum includes several giant "barns" that house inoperable trains, which kids peek into for a view of past train travel. The highlight is boarding a train for a ride.

Unfortunately, when my family and I visited we found it difficult to find information about when trains were scheduled to depart. Also, some train rides are longer than others so make sure to ask about the length of the ride before you jump on board. The cafeteria provides outside and indoor dining. A gift shop features a large kids' section stocked with *Thomas* supplies and two train tables for kids to play with. Admission is $8 for adults, $6 for children ages 5 to 11, and free for children under five. The maximum a family is charged for admittance is $30—so bring the whole gang! It is open mid-April through late October, but call ahead to confirm near the beginning or end of the season. The bathrooms are clean and large. Parking is free.

Kiddieland

8400 West North Avenue   www.kiddieland.com
Melrose Park
708-343-8000

For more than three decades Kiddieland has provided fun for the littlest thrill-seeker. Kiddieland offers amusement park rides for the youngest of kids—18 months and older. There are great rides for older kids, which include the log jammer with a 35-foot drop that my four-year-old loves! The park is small and very manageable with young children. The food is what you would expect— hotdogs, pizza and ice cream. Admission is steep but worth the expense at $19 for adults and children six and older; $16 for children three to five years old and free for children two and younger. The park is open during warm weather months, typically from mid-April through October on weekends. The park is open weekdays from early June through August. The bathroom facilities are a challenge. Each facility is small, with a shared entrance/exit, which makes it difficult to maneuver in and out of, let alone with a stroller. Parking is free.

Kohl Children's Museum

*165 Green Bay Road   www.kohlchildrensmuseum.org
Wilmette
847-512-1300

Kohl Children's Museum is a terrific destination for young toddlers through preschool-age kids. The play grocery store is the best of any museum in the area. There are plenty of terrific imagination-stirring exhibits, such as a boat that kids fish from, a house to build and construction equipment that really works. The museum also has a great music exhibit complete with recording machines for children to record and play back tunes they create. Upstairs in "Grandma's Attic" there are dress up clothes, interconnected barrels for children to crawl through and a fabulous art space, in which projects are process-oriented. There is a small café where healthy items and treats are sold. Now, if it could only expand the bathrooms (only two toilets and a baby changing station in the women's rooms) it would be the perfect destination. Admittance is $6 for adults and children. Children less than one are admitted for free. There is a free, small parking lot.

*Kohl Children's Museum is moving into a spectacular new facility at The Glen in Glenview. The new museum will open in October 2005 and feature phenomenal indoor exhibits, which Kohl is known for and great outdoor areas for families to explore too. Some of the highlights include

"Street Scape," a kid-sized town complete with a grocery store, café, pet/veterinarian clinic, a library and a car shop. The museum will have a new water exhibit, three times the size of the current one. The indoor water exhibit will have levers and valves that kids manipulate to control outdoor water fountains. The outdoor area will include a play space, gardens, painting walls, hiking paths and nature trails. The building will have "LEED Silver Certification," which means it is earth-friendly. The entire building is handicapped accessible. The new museum will be double the current size, have a larger café and many more free parking spaces. And, yes, there will be many more bathrooms! I cannot wait for it to open. In fact, I think this new museum calls for having another child so that I can fully enjoy all it will offer for many years to come!

Mystic Waters Family Aquatic Center
2025 Miner Street
Des Plaines
847-391-5705

Mystic Waters is a fun pool and water park for kids of all ages. Younger children enjoy a ride down the lazy river on large floats (supplied by the water park) with mom or dad. The zero-depth pool is great for babies, toddlers and young swimmers. Older children love Otter's Run, which includes twisting, thrilling water slides. A small concession shop offers hot dogs, pizza and ice cream, but no healthy options. Families who bring their own food coolers must leave them in a designated area for snacking. The pool is extremely clean, as are the locker rooms and bathrooms. Admission is $8 for adults, $7 for children and children less than two years are admitted for free. Parking is free and plentiful.

Wonder Works
6445 West North Avenue   www.wonder-works.org
Oak Park
708-383-4815

Wonder Works is a new museum that opened in 2003. It is an ideal destination for toddlers and preschoolers especially for parents who must keep track of more than one child. There are several main exhibits, which include the Great Outdoors, Lights, Camera, Action, (in which your child is the star or the camera operator), a fantastic process-oriented art room and a building area with many types of blocks and tools. Coming soon is a Farm to Market exhibit. Wonder Works is a great stress-free destination. Admittance is $5 a person, kids or adults. The museum is open Wednesday, Friday and Saturday from 10:00 AM–5:00 PM and Thursday's from 10:00 AM–8:00 PM. There's a small parking lot and ample street parking. No food is sold at the museum. The bathrooms are small, but adequate.

The End

About the Author

Shana Trombley is a southerner by birth but a Chicagoan by choice. Before moving to Chicago, Shana received a BS in political science from the University of Colorado at Boulder. Since 1993 she has lived in Chicago. Shana worked in public affairs before having children. More recently she served as the co-director of the Northside Parents Network. Shana and her husband, Steve, have two children, Abby, seven years and Peter, four years.

About the Cover Designer

Deb is a proud Chicagoan, wife, and mother to Jane, three, and Eden, one. Working part-time as a graphic designer from her Andersonville home, she caters to non-profit organizations and small businesses.

About the Illustrator

Abby Trombley just completed first grade. She loves horseback riding, swimming, drawing and playing with her friends.